OUR SIDE IS RIGHT

LONDON : HUMPHREY MILFORD

OXFORD UNIVERSITY PRESS

OUR SIDE IS RIGHT

BY

RALPH BARTON PERRY

CAMBRIDGE, MASSACHUSETTS
HARVARD UNIVERSITY PRESS
1942

CONTENTS

CONTENTS

OUR SIDE IS RIGHT

CHAPTER I

OUR SIDE IS RIGHT

THE friend of victory will build bridges, and not dig ditches, between those who are fighting with him on the same side. The antidote to division is the conviction of the rightness of the common cause. There are two teachings that are widely diffused in our time, and which can be allowed, or deliberately used, to weaken such conviction.

The first of these is the teaching that convictions do not matter. It is simple-minded — so the argument runs — to suppose that historical events are deliberately planned. Tolstoy is cited as an authority, to show that Napoleon's defeat in Russia was due not to the greatness of Prince Kutuzov but to the inevitable trend of things. Great men do not make history, but are made by history. They are fortunate enough to profit by a collective will which moves the mass of mankind. They simply sense its direction and fall into step at the head of the column.

The application to the present crisis is evident. The rise of the Axis menace is not the work of Hitler, or of Mussolini, or of Hirohito. It is not to be explained by the ideas which these nations or their leaders profess. It is the result of historical forces of which these leaders are merely the puppets and the profiteers. It is false, therefore, to blame either these leaders or their ideas. They are being swept along by the tide. Those who would resist them, like America and the other United Nations, will recognize that it is idle to oppose this sort of cosmic surge. The best that can be done is to climb onto the driver's seat and seize the steering wheel. Then it is possible that one can alter the direction — slightly. But even this is not clear. According to the strict letter of the doctrine, steering wheels are not in order at all. Events are sweeping by and one gets aboard, merely displacing those already there, or asking them to move over.

That this teaching tends to weaken moral

conviction needs no proving. It is impossible to hold convictions firmly and at the same time to be persuaded that they make no practical difference. Those who are really persuaded that moral convictions exert no power over external events proceed to narrow the sphere of morals to their own inner consciousness, where they *can* exert power. The two things are inseparable — the conviction of what ought to be, and the confident effort to bring it to pass.

This doctrine of the impotence of individuals and ideas is seductive because it saves one from the pains of making moral decisions and the greater pains of putting them into practice. It is easier to mount on a "wave" than to swim: since it saves one the trouble of choosing a destination and of propelling oneself towards it. And if Goebbels wanted to weaken our convictions he would seek to persuade us first that history is made by waves, and second that the Axis powers are on the crest of the present wave. Then, having seen the folly of resistance, we would conclude that much the easiest and most sensible thing was to become a fellow-traveller.

This doctrine is not only dangerous to our convictions, and hence to our hope of success, but discredited and false. It is the old idea of fate dressed up in modern clothes. It was revived in the nineteenth century to offset the overconfidence of the eighteenth century. Fate is simply a name for those causes which we do not understand, or which are so complex that mechanisms have not yet been devised for their control. Weather, for example, is still accepted as a fatality.

Tolstoy was a great novelist, but he was not a scientist. His account of Napoleon's Russian campaign is a hodgepodge of agnosticism, fatalism, piety, patriotism, and hero-worship. He tells us that great historical events are *not* caused by "the will of a single man"; they come about "step by step, event by event, moment by moment," "as the result of an infinite number of heterogeneous conditions." It is impossible to answer the question "when Moscow was abandoned"; and as to the return to Moscow, "the Russian army . . . could have done nothing else." Greater than the "great" are those "solitary men who, being able to comprehend the will of Providence, subordinate their own wills to it." Such was Prince Kutuzov, whom the will of Providence had apparently appointed its agent for "the salvation and glory of Russia." But then, finally, it appears that Kutuzov was peculiarly qualified for this assignment because he refused to identify the salvation of Russia with the defense of Moscow; because he alone "understood the meaning of what was taking place"; and because, knowing the condition of both armies, he fitted his action (or inaction) to the times and circumstances and to the requirements of grand strategy![1]

Those who pride themselves on their "realistic" view of history oscillate between the extreme of practicality and the extreme of mysticism. Attacking utopianism, they insist that ideals are worthless unless they can be translated into action and that if they are to be translated into action they must take ac-

[1] Leo Tolstoy, *War and Peace*, vol. V, part xiii, chapters i and ii; vol. VI, part xv, chapters iv and xi. The translation here quoted is that published by the Thomas Y. Crowell Co., New York, 1898–99.

count of actual conditions. This restricts the number of ideals from which choice is made to those which can be implemented, but otherwise leaves the ideals themselves undetermined. To derive these also from reality it is necessary to find "trends" in history, such as "dynamism" and "revolution," which owe what plausibility they possess to their lack of meaning. They amount to no more than saying that history is change, which is self-evident and redundant; or they are invested with a vague sense of direction and destination which reflects the bias of the author.[2]

The lesson to be learned from nazi Germany and her more apt pupils is the precise opposite of the doctrine of fate. The Germans have so developed the technical arts, and the power of coördinating them, that they are in fact remaking Europe with a blueprint. The development of the most formidable war machine in human history, the timing of aggressions, the depopulation of

[2] Cf. Lawrence Dennis, *The Dynamics of War and Revolution*, 1940.

Poland, the destruction of the Jews, the integration of Central Europe, and the construction of an economic bloc based on barter, are not the results of any primal and inscrutable urge which happened to *emerge* in the fourth decade of the twentieth century. They are the achievements of highly intelligent men who know what they want and devise the necessary means. These men do not underestimate the difficulties. *Because* they understand that knowledge and control are inseparable, they avail themselves of the latest and fullest knowledge. Because they recognize the importance of the will of the "masses" they have developed to an unparalleled degree the art of creating that will by propaganda. They hold that history is made by an "élite," whose powers and privileges they claim for themselves. And one of their most effective methods of making history is to persuade the other élite who might oppose them that history is not made by men but men by history.

❈   ❈   ❈

The second way of weakening men's moral convictions is to convince them that all moral convictions are equally right. For it is almost impossible, despite a large capacity for self-contradiction, that men should hold a definite moral conviction and at the same time harbor the idea that the opposite conviction is equally valid.

Here the Axis ideologists find us extremely vulnerable. We believe in freedom and tolerance, and is it not a corollary of freedom and tolerance to respect the other man's belief even though it be a belief in slavery and intolerance? In short, the more pure and scrupulous the liberal is the more surely can he be counted on to befriend the enemies of liberalism. And once these are morally befriended, and their code is given an equal standing with our own, it becomes ridiculous to fight them on moral grounds. There may still be other things to fight about, such as life, property, and territory, but the moral motivation is gone.

* * *

It is very important to clear up this muddle. For muddle it is. It arises from a failure to distinguish between a moral difference and a merely emotional difference. There is a moral difference between ourselves and the nazis because we believe that freedom is right, and they believe that slavery is right. Both beliefs cannot be true, and whichever is true is true for any believer, whether he be American or nazi. If we say, "Freedom is right" and the nazis say "Slavery is right," and if we then say, "Their opinion is just as true as ours," we talk nonsense; precisely as though we were to say, "We believe that 2 plus 2 is 4, they believe that 2 plus 2 is 5, and their judgment is as true as ours."

Either a moral judgment *is* a judgment, and as such debatable, or it is merely an emotional expression of the person who utters it. There is no possible escape from universal criteria of truth unless one is prepared to say, for example, that "Justice is right" means absolutely nothing more than "I am in favor of justice." No moral relativist has ever been relativistic enough to take this position and adhere to it consistently. As an actual force in modern thought, moral relativism is a confused idea the genesis of which belongs to the pathology of the human mind.

If "right" is to be used as the predicate of a sentence which is true or false, then "right" must have a meaning. In spite of the moral skepticism which has run riot in the world during the last century there is little disagreement as to what that meaning is. The right act is the act that best satisfies all claims as they are viewed by a disinterested and sympathetic observer. If two people need food, and there is only one loaf available, it is right to divide the loaf rather than give it all to one. Slavery is wrong because it totally ignores the claims of the slave. Freedom is right because it gives to each as fully as is consistent with giving to all. This is not the whole of morality, but is its central core — whether it be expressed in the Golden Rule, or the standard of justice, or the gospel of love, or the goal of social welfare. When right is given this meaning then the question whether an act or policy is right becomes a question to which there is a theoretically ascertainable answer — and an answer on which all who follow the evidence are bound to agree.

*   *   *

Hitler himself takes "idealistic" grounds. In addressing the Reichstag on September 13, 1935, he said:

"These 68 millions of men could never be governed by commands, as they could by an appeal to their inner instincts, an appeal to their conscience. . . . The strength of idealism alone has accomplished these acts which have moved the world. . . . You have all felt this in the past, for to every single one of you at some time has occurred the reflection that *it is no subtlety of the intellect, but rather an inner voice that has at some time given its commands to every one of you. Reason must have dissuaded you from coming to me; faith alone gave you the command.* What idealism it was — but what a force lay in that idealism!" [3]

[3] Adolf Hitler, "Speech to the Reichstag, Nuremberg, September 13, 1935," *My New Order,* ed. by Raoul de Roussy de Sales, 1941, pp. 337–38. Quoted by permission of Reynal and Hitchcock, publishers.

But in the sense in which Hitler here uses the term, idealism may be moral or immoral. Once it is understood that a thing is not made right simply because of the emotion it excites, then it follows that a man or a nation may be passionately devoted to the wrong. It then becomes possible to say that what *we* call right *is* right, while what the Germans call right is *wrong*, despite the fact that they are just as deeply moved by their wrong as we by our right. In other words let us give the Devil his due. The Devil has his own cause — his pride of power — to which he is passionately and consistently devoted. He heartily hates God, and hates him for his goodness. He knows how to mask himself, and how to divide the followers of righteousness against one another. He gathers other fallen angels about him, establishes himself as their leader, and infuses them with a collective hate of God to which they are prepared to subordinate their personal interests.

It is to be noted that when the Axis ideologists show a "decent respect for the opinions of mankind" they use the same vocabulary as ours. They complain of the injustices which they have received, encourage the aspirations of oppressed peoples, and boast of a classless society. But they have another code which they both profess at home and practice abroad. The best single name for this code is *tribalism* — the supreme exaltation of a particular racial group. The German folk, a nation-state united by common blood, is taken as the ultimate standard and authority. This tribal entity creates obligations, but has none — either to its individual members or to the rest of mankind. It is a colossal ego which affirms itself, and against which there is no appeal. In relation to the tribe, the individual has duties of loyalty, discipline, self-sacrifice, and military valor. But the tribe itself has no duties whatever. It is a law unto itself, and the ruler of the tribe, whether he be a hereditary monarch or a self-appointed Führer, speaks in the name of the tribe and claims the same immunity. In refusing to acknowledge any claims other than its own this tribal idealism violates the very essence of morality.

To admit that the cause of tribalism is as right as that which we adopt not only robs us of our own convictions but amounts to an acceptance of the enemy's. For if one cause is no better than another, or is right in no sense that is not equally applicable to its opposite, the terms "better" and "right" are divested of any moral meaning. The ultimate appeal is to force. For "better" is substituted "stronger," and the evidence is survival and expansion. In order that this test may be applied it is necessary that the rival causes should resort to war; and war, instead of being a calamity or relic of barbarism, assumes the role of the final tribunal before which all international disputes are adjudicated. At best this is a revival of the Teutonic "ordeal by battle," in which victory in combat is accepted as a test of justice or of divine favor. At worst it means a return to the primitive practice of fighting out a quarrel without regard to its merits. It implies that the quarrels of war have no merits.

❊   ❊   ❊

There are two ways of persuading us that as between the enemy's cause and our cause there is no moral difference. The first is to prove that theirs is as good as ours, since theirs is theirs as ours is ours, both being pursued with the same loyalty and devotion. This is the doctrine of the relativity of creeds, and is designed to appeal to our sympathy and our liberalism: Love thy neighbor's creed as thine own! The second way of equalizing the two creeds is to say that ours is as bad as theirs. This appeals to our cynicism or sense of guilt.

The present war, it is said, is a war between imperialisms, one old and the other new, but otherwise the same. Who are we of the United Nations to preach morality? Are we not guilty of every imperialistic crime? Should we not first cast the beam out of our own eye before attempting to pull the mote out of our brother's? Or, since both parties are imperialists, why not wash one's hands of the whole business and let the guilty destroy one another? Or, why not frankly admit that all eyes have beams and motes, and nobody

is guilty? Admitting that we are no less imperialistic than they, we can come to terms;
or having got rid of all hypocrisy, we can then
fight it out honestly and let the stronger possess the earth.

That Britain and the United States have
both been guilty of imperialism is, of course,
true. But by what *standard* are they guilty?
To which the answer is, their own standard.
There are two ways of condemning these old
imperialisms. They can be condemned by the
jealousy and covetousness of new imperialisms — by the have-nots who would like to
have, and to enter in their turn upon a new
phase of aggrandizement and exploitation.
But they can also be condemned, as they have
been condemned, from within, by those of
their own people who would like to rid the
world of imperialism altogether.

No American should be allowed to forget
that although we fought for our independence
against the hated "redcoats" and their "hired
Hessians," the ideas which inspired that
struggle, and which were embodied in the
American Declaration of Independence and

the bill of rights, were the ideas of English-
men. Precisely the same thing has happened
in the later evolution of the British Empire
into the British Commonwealth of Nations.
Those whose conscience was most offended
by the British conquest of the Boers were men
like John Morley and the "Little Englanders,"
or their American cousins. Australia, New
Zealand, South Africa, and Canada have become free nations without wars of independence because their peoples are imbued with
the Anglo-Saxon traditions of liberty, and because the British Government has had to
reckon with the libertarian sympathies of its
own people. And the same is true of Ireland
— for, despite the cruelties and blunders of
the British Government, the most powerful
force for Irish freedom has been the fact that
modern Britain could not treat Ireland as
Germany has treated Poland without violat-
ing the sentiments of her own people.

The Indian Agent General at Washington
said, in defending his people's right to independence, that they have been nourished on
the literature of freedom introduced by their

British rulers. To me the most impressive and
heartening words in Sir Stafford Cripps's
parting broadcast to the people of India were
these:

"No responsible Indian has questioned the
sincerity of our main purpose — complete
freedom for India. Such an effort inspired
by good-will and sincerity will leave its mark
on the history of our relations and will cast
its beneficent light forward into the future
— it will prove to have been the first step
along the path of freedom for India and of
friendship between our two countries." [4]

The same pattern of development has been
followed in our own briefer imperialistic ca-
reer. We have transformed a Monroe Doctrine into a Good Neighbor Policy. We have
given our dependencies independence — not
because we could not have held them in subjection, but because such a policy would have
been inconsistent with our institutions and
with the traditional creed of Americans. We
conquered Aguinaldo despite the protests of

[4] *Boston Herald*, Sunday, April 12, 1942, p. 17, col. 4.

our anti-imperialists, but though the anti-imperialists of 1898 were derided as sentimentalists and were outshouted and outvoted at
the time, it is their spirit rather than that of
the jingo majority that fought so memorably
on the Bataan Peninsula.

Let us grant that western imperialism is
suffering in this hour of crisis from its past
sins. The important fact is that the sense of
its *moral* bankruptcy is felt most keenly by
the Anglo-Saxon conscience itself. To our
enemies western imperialism is merely weak,
needing to be strengthened by a change of
masters and a new technique of mastery. To
the Anglo-Saxon mind it is wrong, and needs
to be transformed into a new and more radi-
cal system of freedom.

I am not interested in claiming a monopoly
of the tradition of freedom for English-speak-
ing countries. Chapters of the literature of
freedom are written in every tongue and in-
scribed in the hearts of men of every nation.
The rapid shrinking of the world has spread
the infection wide, and brought a growing
conviction that there can be no lasting free-

dom anywhere without freedom everywhere. In a world which is now, for better or for worse, one world — not only in theory and before God, but in the every-day practical experience of its human inhabitants — we have today to decide which it shall be, the better or the worse. The worse way is to subject the whole of that world to one of its parts — to whatever part may be bold and powerful enough to achieve and hold the mastery. The better way is to create a federation of the whole which is stronger than any of the parts, and which may preserve peace and promote coöperation among them.

The rise of the nazi and Axis power has forced this issue. It drives us to choose between a worse evil and a better good than mankind has ever known before. We must be visionary and utopian if we are not to be unprecedentedly base; in order to be realistic we must be loftily idealistic. But this moral ideal has long been working in us. It is humanism, Christianity, liberalism, and democracy, carried to their logical conclusions. It means having the courage of our humane,

Christian, liberal, and democratic convictions. It means attending to the unfinished business which was long ago included in our agenda. Most certainly we have a right to call it ours.

CHAPTER II

DEMOCRACY AT THE CROSS ROADS

From the standpoint of Americans the present war is the supreme ordeal of democracy, which is to determine whether or not "the world of tomorrow" shall be a world in which a democracy can not only survive, but flourish and realize its destiny. It is appropriate therefore that in this grave hour we should take account of our weakness and our strength *as* a democracy. To what dangers does our democracy expose us, and how shall we as a democracy find the power to meet those dangers? First, then, what *is* democracy?

If we look beyond the habits and mechanisms of democracy, beyond equalitarian manners and forms of speech, beyond manhood suffrage and the rule of the majority, to its original and perennial spring, we discover its attitude to man. Democracy focuses attention on the manhood of men, and finds that manhood worthy of attention. With this as our key we shall be able to understand both the weaknesses of democracy and its strength.

Taking men in the concrete one may notice their individual differences, or one may notice their common aspect of humanity. This, however, does not suffice to distinguish democracy. Shakespeare, who avoided taking sides, saw man as ridiculous in the "strange eventful history" of the seven ages from infancy to second childhood and oblivion; but also recorded another, and equally authentic, feeling when he put into Hamlet's mouth the famous apostrophe:

"What a piece of work is a man! how noble in reason! how infinite in faculty! in form and moving how express and admirable! in action how like an angel! in apprehension how like a God! the beauty of the world! the paragon of animals!"

Then, having depicted man so glowingly, Hamlet could say in the next breath, "And

yet, to me, what is this quintessence of dust?
Man delights not me." [1] The ancients defined
man as a rational and god-like being; but
also as a two-legged animal without feathers,
and (to distinguish him from a plucked cock)
with broad flat nails.[2]

Man is, in fact, both admirable and con-
temptible. He has two sides, the upper and
the lower, and democracy sees the upper, the
side that faces toward God. Disraeli, referring to the controversy raging over evolution,
put the question, "Is man an ape or an
angel?" and answered that he was "on the
side of the angels." [3] Democracy is, with
Disraeli, on the side of the angels.

But to say that democracy uses the term
"man" in the eulogistic rather than the derog-
atory sense does not yet suffice. Nietzsche,
who deplored man's all-too-human traits,
nevertheless credited man with a power to
surpass himself.

[1] *Hamlet*, Act II, Scene 2.
[2] Diogenes Laertius, *Lives and Opinions of Philosophers,* translated by Yonge, *Diogenes,* 6.
[3] *Speech at Oxford, Diocesan Conference,* Nov. 25,
1864.

"What is the ape to man? A laughing-stock, a thing of shame. And just the same shall man be to the Superman: a laughing-stock, a thing of shame." [4]

Thus man may be admired for what he is at his best, at the upper limit of his attainment, or as the forerunner of a higher race. And this selective or prophetic admiration may be accompanied by a contempt for actual men in the mass. Democracy, on the other hand, invests every man with some shred of that which dignifies the best man — dwelling on every man's possession of the same god-like faculties, or on the possibility of every man's redemption.

Even this, however, will not suffice, though it is as far as the pagan view of man will carry us. To understand the democratic attitude it is necessary to find good in every man, not symbolically, vicariously, or even potentially, but in his actual condition. At this point modern democracy has assimilated the Christian

[4] *Thus Spake Zarathustra*, tr. by Thomas Common, Macmillan, 1911, part i, Prologue, § 3. Quoted by permission of the publishers.

teaching of charity. The Christian God loves
men not for the perfections which they pre-
figure and occasionally attain, but for that
incompleteness and capacity for suffering
which is the common lot. He loves them as a
parent loves his children — because they need
him. When the Christian God became man
in order to complete his divinity, he was born
in a manger and died on a cross. The humanity of God and the divinity of man both lie in
humility, aspiration, and struggle.

This insistence on the equal dignity and
loveworthiness of men has led to a distortion
of the true meaning of democracy. Arising as
a protest against pride and the exaggerated
esteem of superiors, it dwells on the humanity
of men at the bottom of the scale.

> Ye see yon birkie, ca'd a lord,
>   Wha struts and stares, and a' that;
> Tho' hundreds worship at his word,
>   He's but a coof for a' that.

To raise the man below, the poet brings down
the man above. In this revolutionary phase
the praise of man becomes a praise of "honest poverty" — of those who dine on "homely

fare" and wear "hodden-gray," of "the pith o' sense, and pride o' worth" that are possessed by men who possess nothing else.[5]

But a democracy which has recovered its balance will feel its respect for men universally. It will see the dignity of manhood and the pathos of human life in all men equally, and will dispense its unbiased charity to the rich and the poor, to the wise and the ignorant, the powerful and the weak.

The core of modern democracy consists, then, in an attitude which comprises these three things: the acknowledgment of the manhood of each and every human individual; a respect for the generic essence of manhood, however slight its traces, as comprising those faculties of reason and conscience through which the light of truth finds its way into the natural world; and finally an all-compassing and compassionate love of individual men as seekers after truth, stumbling in the half-darkness, frustrated by obstacles, and suffering alternations of happiness and misery, hope and despair.

Democracy so conceived is consistent with

[5] Robert Burns, "Is There For Honest Poverty."

the root-idea of morality, and develops its fuller social implications, being founded on a disinterested acknowledgment of all human claims, and their right to maximum fulfillment. It is the form of social organization that can be said to be right in a universal sense. The further particularities of democracy are entailed in this moral essence: the equal dignity of men as man; the duty of organized society to serve the happiness of its people; the authority of the private reason and conscience over public institutions; the rights and liberties by which this duty and this authority are guaranteed and made effectual; the goal of universal fraternity and peace; the hope of progress — progress in truth and in well-being, and progress for all.

*   *   *

Of the three great hazards to which democracy is exposed the first arises from the very splendor of its vision. It asks too much. It addresses to every man the counsel which Marcus Aurelius reserved for the sage: "If a thing is possible and proper to men, deem it attainable by thee." [6] The vision of democracy is not irrelevant to man — it is profoundly human; every form and value of life which it envisages falls within the limits of some human experience and corresponds to some element of human nature. But it asks all men all the time to be at their best, and so while it expresses the possibilities of human nature it violates its actualities and goes against the grain. Its realization in a large-scale society involves such complexities and intricate adjustments, such delicacies of feeling, and such depths of wisdom, as to exceed men's normal capacity. It creates new evils of the very sort which it is designed to correct; and although proposed as a form of social organization, it appears to conflict with the basic conditions of social organization.

Thus democracy proclaims equality, and yet it encourages men to take full advantage of their natural inequalities. It offers all men equally the opportunity to rise in life, and then since they are unequally endowed they rise to unequal heights. Social organization

[6] *Meditations*, VI.

requires leadership and control, in both the economic and political fields, but democracy encourages men to resist authority, and to prolong discussion at the expense of unified action. Social organization requires restraint, but democracy finds difficulty in drawing a line between the rights of freedom and the abuses of license. Democracy exalts the role of the individual, but social organization requires a common basis of agreement in order that men may live and work together. To win their way in the world men and societies require conviction, but democracy preaches tolerance and the open mind. And although individual attainment depends on ambition, and the social life is enriched by rivalry and competition, democracy, like Christianity, preaches unselfishness and mutual help.

The half-truths of democracy are easier to grasp and to follow than the whole truth. And these half-truths tend to war against one another, and thus to divide democracy into opposing forces each of which takes the ground of democracy and uses its symbols.

Democracy has its solutions of these difficulties. It is possible to reconcile a spirit of equal respect with a recognition of differences in talent and attainment. It is possible to follow leaders and obey authorities, of one's own free choosing; and, by limiting one's own freedom, to make room for the freedom of others. It is possible for diverse individuals to come to agreement, and to set limits of time to discussion. It is possible for men to believe and yet listen, and to identify their personal ambitions and rivalries with the public good. These whole truths are possible, but they are hard — so hard, indeed, that they must be considered as goals rarely and only imperfectly attained. Democracy thus becomes a standard or norm rather than an actual mode of behavior; which is not to belittle it, but rather to place it with the Golden Rule, the Ten Commandments, the two great commandments, and every other counsel of perfection designed to direct men's endeavor and measure their shortcomings.

An unattainable ideal tends in the long run, however, to produce sentimentalism and hypocrisy. Too great a gap between the reach and the grasp, or between the star and the wagon, leads to subjective compensations. Men tend to substitute the wish for the will, the feeling for the achievement, the word for the deed. Weary of straining to attain a distant and elusive goal, they create mirages or shut their eyes to their actual position. Sentimentalism and hypocrisy in turn produce a revulsion of feeling. Men scornfully reject the ideal, and pride themselves on their realism. From this soul-sickness spring cynicism and pessimism, or a readiness to accept some new gospel as different as possible from the old.

✳   ✳   ✳

The second hazard of democracy is its vulnerability to external force. To understand this hazard it is first necessary to disabuse oneself of a superstition that is especially widespread among men of conscience and piety. It might be described as the idealist's occupational disease. I refer to the belief that good will somehow prevail over evil by its sheer goodness — that good, in short, is a sort of power.

I do not deny that good *will* prevail over

evil — that is a faith which I share with all other moral idealists. I mean only to point out that if the good does prevail it will prevail not through its own intrinsic essence but through the good men, or gods, or angels in whom it is embodied. Good, like evil, will prevail only if its adherents are its champions, possessing weapons and knowing how to use them: weapons fit to cope with the weapons of the enemy on the field of battle. I do not refer merely to war in the strict sense. The good will prevail in the world of existence only if it satisfies the conditions of existence. The prevailing of good over evil does not mean merely that good is better than evil — *that* it is by definition; it means that good men and good societies are stronger than evil men and evil societies. If the embodiments of good are to survive and prevail they must be strong in body, and exert bodily force to meet whatever bodily force may be brought against them.

I have been reading a book by Eugene Bagger in which the author, a convert to catholicism, relates his personal pilgrimage from Cnossus to Canossa. Cnossus was the capital of Crete when, in the second millennium before Christ, Crete was the center of the Minoan Empire. Of all historic cities, says our author, Cnossus most nearly anticipated modern New York. Then he adds:

"And all that splendor, all that beauty, all that ingenious planning and managing of common human happiness, came to an end over-night. Cnossus, and all it stood for, was destroyed as a mighty tree is destroyed by a stroke of lightning." [7]

"Cnossus and all it stood for" — its beauty, its wisdom, its happiness; New York, America, and all they stand for — their hope of a better life for the masses of men, their purpose to achieve a free Christian society: a stroke of brutal force may destroy them over-night unless that force is met with like force, on the same causal plane and in the same space and time.

This may seem to neglect religion. On the contrary. Men have invoked God not be-

[7] *For the Heathen are Wrong*, 1941, p. 6. Quoted by permission of the publishers, Little, Brown and Company.

cause they thought that good was invulnerable to force, but because, recognizing the exposure of good and its precarious foothold, their faith supplied a needed counterforce. The God of religion is not pure Goodness, but a being who unites with his goodness of will a control of nature — an omnipotence which can meet the lightning with thunderbolts of its own.

As Christianity is humanized the "power not ourselves that makes for righteousness" is removed from the Heavens and becomes more closely identified with the moral will incarnate in the race of men. The transcendent God of mediaeval Christianity, and the peripheral God of deism — the God who first created and thereafter occasionally intervened — is superseded by the God who works continuously through evolution and history. But whether God be remote or immanent he works upon and through the same agencies as those with which men build cities and protect them: through the intelligent and beneficent control of physical causes.

The city of man, or the city of God on

earth, may, then, be destroyed by lightning and can be preserved only by insulation or by counterstrokes of more destructive lightning. For lightning substitute war. There is no difference, except that war is lightning forged and launched by men. The city and all it stands for can be defended against war only by withdrawal or by counter-war. As withdrawal becomes impossible in a compact and teeming world, counter-war becomes the only effective means by which war, once war has been launched, can be effectively met and the city saved.

So inescapable is this truth that it may be said to be the central truth of the moral life: to act for good ends with material means; to realize the good in terms of existence; and then to protect this creation, compounded of real and ideal, against those hazards which it encounters on the level of reality — hazards which may spring from inanimate forces or from forces which are animated by contrary ideals.

This is both the central truth of the moral life and also its tragic predicament. For the enemies which the moral will encounters have to be met on their own ground. They may take the initiative and dictate the weapons to be used. Hence men of good will may find themselves compelled to choose between surrender and the use of the most repugnant methods. To seize property in order that men may enjoy property; to take life in order to make life secure; to deprive men of liberty in order to create liberty; to cut in order to heal; to break law in order to make law; to hurt in order to remove pain; to make war in order to bring peace: these are, if you like, paradoxes; but they are necessary paradoxes. They are inherent in the nature of human life; and they are conspicuous in the heroic periods of human history and in great men of action — Pericles, Charlemagne, St. Louis, Henry IV, William of Orange, Cromwell, Washington, Lincoln.

In democracy this paradox exists in its most acute form. Unquestionably war is profoundly contrary to the genius of democracy; and as war has developed in craft and brutality, in its wholesale destructiveness, and in its absorption of the total energies of society this paradox has grown progressively more acute. Christian democracy teaches men to look upon their enemies as brothers; but war has now lost almost every vestige of generosity, of chivalry, or even of honor. Democracy teaches men to respect the individual person; modern war puts a premium on solidarity. Democracy accustoms men to persuasion, while war inflames, threatens and intimidates. Democracy is pledged to enlightenment; modern war has found a new and formidable weapon in the organized and methodical propagation of lies. Democracy is a cult of freedom, war requires discipline. Democracy preserves happiness, war teaches hardness and insensibility. Democracy dreams of a fellowship of nations exchanging goods, services and cultures for their mutual enrichment; war begets conquest and exploitation.

Democracy, in short, unfits its adherents for war. It disarms its own soldiers. Hating and renouncing war, and unwilling even to admit its possibility, democracy is caught unawares and suffers defeats before it can achieve victories.

This problem, too, has its solution. It is humanly possible to engage in war in order to eradicate its hateful practices. There is no logical contradiction between war and peace unless they are both adopted as ultimate ends. There remains the psychological question: whether a man can engage in war and still at the bottom of his heart reject it. He can, but it is difficult. There are soldiers who can hate war and remain good soldiers. There is a clear difference between the sadist who enjoys killing, or the militarist who esteems the military virtues above all other values, and the man who fights reluctantly as the only means to save his home or country or the opportunity to devote himself to peaceful vocations. But for our enemies it is a simpler matter. With the Japanese follower of Bushido, the German nazi, or the Italian fascist, the qualities which fit men for war — hardness, discipline, physical aggressiveness and the taking of life — enjoy the highest sanctions of conscience and religion. The adherent of democracy, on the other hand, has to distinguish between his fundamental code of peace and the necessities of war. Hence the transition from peace to war is retarded. He suffers an inner conflict during the period of war. And when war is over he returns eagerly to the ways of peace, only to be caught unprepared should war be again forced upon him.

✳   ✳   ✳

The first and second of the hazards of democracy pave the way to the third. Discouraged by his shortcomings and by his weakness against external enemies, the adherent of democracy grows skeptical and is vulnerable to heresy. Having lost faith in his own gods he is tempted to worship false gods.

The present cults of the false gods sprang from seeds sown in the nineteenth century. Of these cults I shall speak of three: primitivism, the gospel of force, and statism or tribalism. Their seeds, sown quite innocently by the science of the last century, were materialism, anti-intellectualism, and social relativism.

By materialism I mean the reduction of

knowledge all along the line in the direction of physics. The development of science in the nineteenth century tended to assimilate chemistry to physics, biology to chemistry, psychology to biology, and man to psychology. Thought of in these terms, man faced backwards toward the womb of nature from which he sprang. His so-called "higher" faculties were analyzed into lower — thought into sense, will into reflex, conscience into emotion. Viewed in the light of the Darwinian struggle for existence, he owed his survival to his physical adaptation, and to his use of "the tooth and the claw" against his competitors.

This train of thought became a heresy when man esteemed himself for that which he had first reluctantly admitted. Ideas which at first only sharpened the distinction between the lower natural and the higher supernatural eventually led to an inversion of values in which the higher became the lower and the lower the higher. Man was admired for that of which he had hitherto been ashamed, and the cult of human dignity gave place to the cults of primitivism and of "blood and soil."

Meanwhile other currents of thought combined with materialism to discredit reason, that faculty for truth which had hitherto been regarded as man's certificate of nobility. Evidence was accumulated to show that man did not live by reason, but by instinct and passion; that the reasons which he gave for his action served only to mask the unreason which really moved him; and that even the theoretical reason was only a form of will, governed by subjective satisfactions rather than by evidence. Psychology was substituted for logic, and propaganda for argument.

This assault upon human reason had in earlier times been used to prove man's need of regeneration or to substitute pessimism for optimism, the standard remaining the same. But anti-intellectualism became a heresy when man praised unreason above reason, darkness above light, the blind surge of will-power or of subterranean drives above the thoughtful adjustment of right means to good ends. Hence the second of the heresies, the worship of blind force.

Meanwhile the spread of science to man focused attention on the social matrix in which the individual is moulded. Society came to be regarded, in the nineteenth century, not as an ideal order in which the life of the human person attains its highest perfection, but as a natural and historical entity into which the human person is absorbed. As a reaction against the older "compact theory" this new way of thinking explained human institutions not as designed to serve man, and therefore as commending themselves to the sober judgment of the individuals living under them, but as greater beings in their own right, causally prior to their individual members. The individual who claims to speak for himself was really only a cell in the body social, a product of social forces, a symptom of his place and time. The integers of human life were now societies, and not men.

This tendency, like materialism and anti-intellectualism, appeared first as a ground for skepticism and pessimism: representing the human individual as hopelessly enmeshed and dependent, and reducing all of his absolutes to relativities. But it is a short step from the recognition of societies as greater beings and overruling causes to their acceptance as standards. This step being taken, the individual no longer contends against the inertia and drift of social life — no longer seeks to bring societies into agreement with truth and good as he sees them; but accepts them as themselves standards of truth and good. The particular society to which he belongs is no longer a state of affairs to be remedied, or a plastic material to be formed after ideal models; but has become his god, to which he surrenders his judgment and his will. The third and last heresy is this worship of the tribe, whether nation, race, or state.

*   *   *

The cure for heresy is the true gospel, or the proof that the false gods are false and their worship superstition. All of these antidemocratic heresies are distorted half-truths or intellectual abortions. No analysis of higher faculties into lower disproves their peculiar and distinctive characteristics. Though dead thought may be dissolved into the dust of sense, or will into reflexes, the fact remains that living thought is different from sensation and living will from reflexes, as a more complex function differs from its constituent elements. That man has emerged from the animal does not shake the fact that he *has* emerged, and emerged into something different. Still less does it prove that this emergent man is not higher than that from which he has emerged.

However the intellect may be corrupted by passion or deflected by prejudice, the intellect still has its own laws. The procedures of intellect in which conclusions are based on evidence still afford the only way to strict truth, however immersed in the context of action. The love of truth, even though it be a kind of love, is still a different kind of love from the love of pleasure or power. To mistake the social causes of ideas for their proofs is sheer confusion. Increase force a thousand times, and it is no better than it was before. The individual is dependent on his social relations both for his existence and for his perfection, but however these relations are multiplied the fact remains that thought, purpose, volition, and love are acts of individuals, and that human life is perfected in persons and not in societies. If a society is not an organization of individuals contributing to the security and enrichment of their personal lives, then it is a mere set of worthless habits. Or if race and state be construed as entities in their own right, then they are either legal fictions or low-grade organisms scarcely meriting admission to the category of animal life, and vastly inferior to the least among their individual members.

*   *   *

If democracy is to be saved, the first and most indispensable condition is that its adherents shall fix their eyes upon it and see it and its rival creeds for what they are. Then to say that the democratic creed is a perfectionism does not argue against it. That is precisely what it is. What more does one want of a creed than that it should create an image of perfection? If the term "democracy" has now become vague, that is not because it means little, but because it means so much.

Democracy is not only a form of government suited to the fullest development of human faculties, and under which individual men may live most proudly; it is not only the form of social life which reflects the widest and most tender compassion; it is also that frame of life within which individual men and groups of men can develop most richly and harmoniously their various gifts and inclinations. It is also that frame of life within which individuals, protected in their freedoms, can engage in the pursuit of the universal values of science, art, and piety, and so contribute to the common fund of culture. It is also that frame of life which permits of the maximum of flexibility and growth, and gives to human history as a whole a direction and a meaning. If there is another and a better name for all these things, I will gladly accept it as a substitute for democracy.

Seeing this vision, it is then necessary to keep the faith. How shall men be induced to keep the faith? By exhortation, by meditation, by prayer, by worship — in short, by religion. Religion is the method by which men are induced to keep to a high purpose which goes against the grain. But even religion will not suffice unless there be some reward for effort — some evidence of salvation. If men are not to be discouraged by the weakness of democracy against external enemies they must acquire the martial virtues and prevail against their foes. They must have a sense of their actual power in time of war, and of their latent power in time of peace. And if men are not to be discouraged by their democratic shortcomings, then they must feel a sense of forward movement. Even though the steps be short, they must *take steps* to be more fully what they profess to be.

If democracy is to survive its present ordeal and live on, the democratic peoples must take the offensive all along the line — the offensive against error, the offensive against external enemies, and the offensive against inertia and reaction within their own house. They must be sustained by conviction of the right, by confidence in their strength, and by hope of attainment.

The advantage of the offensive has its moral as well as its military application. He who takes the offensive selects the time, the place, and the weapons. He who awaits the enemy and fights with his back to the wall has no choice. He cannot even choose the wall. Democracy is now forced to use measures which violate its conscience because it has launched no attacks of its own. It has lost the initiative, and has allowed its foes to present it with the alternatives of subjection or violence.

Being now in that situation, we must fight our way out as best we can. But if we are not to face that situation again we must make our own situation. If we are not to be compelled again to obey a counsel of desperation, we must not only seize the military initiative now at the earliest possible moment, but hold that initiative and translate it in the hour of victory into an attack with political, economic, scientific, and moral weapons on the old unsolved problems of civilization. If we do not relish the methods which any unscrupulous enemy can force us to employ as the price of our lives, then we must wage our own world war, with our own preferred methods of persuasion, humanity, and justice, and ourselves create, after our own model, the world of tomorrow.

CHAPTER III

THE RIGHT AND WRONG OF PROPAGANDA

P<small>ROPAGANDA</small> is used in time of war as a means of creating good morale. We begin, then, with morale. Any description of the actual state of morale soon becomes out of date. Anything written on the subject of American morale before Pearl Harbor was inappropriate the day after Pearl Harbor, and a description written on that date fails to apply to the situation today, when the tide is running strongly against the United Nations, and when a new note of gravity appears in every American utterance, private and public. But the general principles remain the same.

Morale is a familiar experience, with many complex and obscure causes. It would take the combined resources of biology, psychology, psychiatry, and sociology to explain it —

if, indeed, they could explain it. I shall not attempt any such scientific explanation, but shall confine myself to a simple statement of the experience itself and a brief enumeration of the more evident factors by which it can be controlled.

Morale is a state of mind which characterizes groups of men when they are engaged in some joint action; such, for example, as facing an emergency, fighting a battle, or waging a war. Their morale is said to be high when they act together with hearty accord and good will; low, when they are at odds with one another, and sullen or apathetic. High morale may assume many forms according to the circumstances and the phase of action. Every prolonged endeavor has its phases of defense and offense, of preparation and culmination, of quiescence and movement. Hence high morale may show itself in a dashing attack or an orderly retreat, in intensity of effort or in endurance of hardship, in enthusiasm or in cheerfulness and patience. The essence of it is that the group holds together, and holds to its objective, despite

events that are calculated to divide and dis-
hearten.

This state of mind may be controlled, in the
first place, by physical causes. The good officer knows the importance of providing his
men with food, drink, and shelter, and of
hardening their bodies. He knows that if his
men are to suffer physical privations or strain
they must be made to feel that these are reasonable or unavoidable. He must not ask
more of them than they can give, though he
must enable them to give much.

The second control of morale is mental.
The officer need not be a psychologist, but he
will know, perhaps intuitively, how to appeal
to the deeper instincts of the human mind. If
he is a good leader he will know how to
arouse that instinct which disposes men to
follow a leader. He will appeal to affection,
pride, emulation, and combativeness. He
will make routine interesting, and effort ex-
citing. Above all he will know how to appeal
to those elements in human nature which
conduce to *esprit de corps:* the sense of belonging to something honorable and impor-

tant; the sense of participation in collective activity; the sense of rhythm; the sense of rivalry in welldoing.

High morale may be attained on the merely physical and psychological level. The morale of a crack regiment or of a famous ship of war may depend little if at all upon devotion to a cause. Its members may be as ignorant of the purpose of the war or as indifferent to the issues at stake as the members of any other military unit. But the officers have known how to deal with human nature — its physical needs and its general mental capacities. They have known how to make their men cheerful, brave, zealous and proud, with little or no reference to a political or social creed.

War is not waged nor are emergencies met by regiments and ships, but by total societies. The wider *esprit de corps* which embraces an entire nation is called patriotism; and, like the *esprit de corps* of a regiment or ship of war, it may be promoted by physical and psychological causes. But these causes have never been sufficient, especially since the rise of nationalism. A nation feels itself to stand for something, and its unity consists essentially in allegiance to a conception of life which it feels to be superior to that of its rivals.

This third, or ideological, cause of morale is peculiarly imperative in the present crisis. In a recent book entitled *War by Revolution*, one reads that "in this war, which is basically not a war of rival national interests, although national interests enter into it, patriotism is not enough." [1] The participants in the war may be named Germany, Italy, Japan, Great Britain, Russia, China and the United States; but they are also, and with equal propriety, named nazism, fascism, communism, and democracy. The magnitude and uniqueness of the crisis is due to the fact that international and civil conflicts are going on at the same time. For the ideological issues intersect national lines. The nazis are not all in Germany, or the fascists all in Italy, or the communists all in Russia, or the democrats all in the United States. The result is that each nation

[1] Francis Williams, *War by Revolution*, 1941, p. 56.

has at one and the same time to maintain its purely national unity and its integral allegiance to some one of these ideas. It can be weakened and defeated not only by treason, but by heresy. Each nation knows how to exploit this possibility, and to win the support of its ideological sympathizers in the enemy country.

American morale in the present crisis requires, then, something more than devotion to that physical and psychological entity symbolized by the Stars and Stripes; something more than the self-preservative and combative emotions; something more than blind loyalty and heroic self-sacrifice. It requires all of these things, but it requires something more. It requires that we shall be the united and passionate adherents of the democratic creed, and that our people shall be satisfied with that creed as promising a solution of their problems and a redress of their grievances. Their loyalty to democracy must be as pure and undivided as their loyalty to their land and their houses, their bodies and their treasures.

✲   ✲   ✲

The fundamental article of democracy is a respect for man, and it seeks so to organize society as to diffuse among its members the maximum of individual enlightenment and liberty. To speak of any given country such as our own as democratic means that its citizens are united in their devotion to this set of related ideas. We do not live up to them, but they define the standard by which we measure our shortcomings. We live *for* them, even if we do not always live by them. We are favorably disposed to them. They exist in us as what we try to be, and blame ourselves for not being. There is a definition of a "Baptist" which is said to be applicable to a certain university whose charter requires that its president shall be an adherent of that denomination. It is said that a Baptist is a man who, when he stays away from church, stays away from the Baptist Church. But this does not fully express the meaning of the definition. He must suffer from self-reproach when he is deficient in Baptist piety. He must be a Baptist in hope, aspiration, and scruple. Similarly, an individual is democratic when he

judges himself by, or suffers from, a democratic personal conscience; and a country is
democratic when its members share a democratic social conscience, despite their in-
fidelities.

This democratic conscience is implanted
in us by all the influences which impinge
upon the individual from his infancy — the
personal influences of family, friends, and
neighbors; the influences of language, books,
newspapers, radio, and cinema; the influences
of legal and political institutions — all of the
myriad influences which in their aggregate
constitute what is called the social environ-
ment. To some extent, these influences are
exerted deliberately — by the teacher, the
writer, the preacher, the political leader, or
as we would now say, the propagandist.

The word "propaganda," like the word
"appeasement," has come to be a name for
the abuse of a useful and indispensable activity. Appeasement means conciliation and
compromise, and is essential not only to
diplomacy, but to all just living. Similarly,
propaganda means influence, or methodi-

cal and organized persuasion, both intellectual and emotional — which are basic social
functions, above all in a democracy. Erasmus
Darwin spoke of Benjamin Franklin as one
"who spread the happy contagion of liberty
among his countrymen." [2] Like other im-
planters of democracy, Franklin formed the
mind of America both by what he was and by
what he taught. He wrote down the ideas of
his age, gave them a happy and alluring expression in his own person, and thus capti-
vated the hearts as well as illuminated the
minds of those exposed to his influence.

Nevertheless, while we know that propaganda goes on continuously — always has,
and always must — we shrink from it. We
employ devices such as town halls, forums,
round tables, and symposiums. We avoid
the word "propaganda"; or stutter and blush
when we use it; or use it only in private
among fellow conspirators. If we have to
refer to it in public, we call it "education,"
"public relations," and "information." We

[2] Quoted by I. Bernard Cohen, *Benjamin Franklin's
Experiments,* 1941, pp. 3–4.

admit that we cannot be one nation without some degree of moral solidarity, and we know that we cannot save ourselves in times of emergency without a heightening of that moral solidarity. But we like to believe that this moral solidarity will somehow take care of itself, without being propagated.

It is imperative that our doubts on this matter of propaganda should be cleared away. Otherwise we shall find ourselves necessarily doing what we disapprove of — doing it with a sense of guilt, and therefore doing it badly, which is certainly no better than doing it well.

       *   *   *

There are two grounds on which we condemn propaganda, both of which, I think, are mistaken. In the first place, we say that emotional appeal is illegitimate, while appeal to reason or experience is legitimate. Thus a recent writer on "Government Propaganda" who properly abhors the thought that we should "out-gabble Goebbels," says:

"It may be that we propagate the gospel of

democracy by the simple process of making available to the people all possible information concerning the workings of their government." [3]

Now the American experts in the German Ministry of Foreign Affairs are better informed concerning the workings of our government than the mass of the American people can ever hope to be; but this information does not convert them to democracy — it only assists them in their determination to destroy it. We are brought back to the fundamental fact that since being democratic consists in being *for* something, it is not propagated when that something is merely described and the description understood. The human mind is quite capable of grasping a fact, an object, or a state of affairs, imaginary or actual, without being either for or against it; and it often occurs that the better it is grasped, the more disfavor it excites, as when Americans acquire information regarding the workings of a nazi government.

According to a second accepted prohibi-

[3] *Atlantic Monthly*, September, 1941, pp. 313, 311.

tion, propaganda must not indoctrinate. We are told that we must not *form* the mind, but simply open it, and keep it open. It was this scruple which led us, before we entered the war, to believe that one side might be presented as emotionally as you liked provided the other side was also presented. A broadcast on the subject of aid to Britain was elevated to the level of an "educational" or "public service" program when it included a speaker who opposed aid to Britain. Thus when an idea was widely accepted its opponents acquired a scarcity value. Men such as Norman Thomas, whose unorthodoxy was not too violent or offensive, were in great demand as professional propaganda disinfectants. They received a hearing out of proportion to what they had to say because in order to appease our social conscience or satisfy our radio regulations it was necessary to have *somebody* say *something* "on the other side"; as a few surviving exponents of the earth-is-flat doctrine might find themselves indispensable in an age which had made up its mind that the earth is round, but felt bound to keep the question open.

It is evident that this clumsy and often absurd device does not go to the root of the matter. If it is wrong to make an emotional appeal, it is no less wrong to make two opposite emotional appeals. If it is wrong to make an emotional appeal in behalf of orthodoxy, the situation is not improved by inviting an emotional appeal in behalf of heresy — especially if the orthodoxy is more probably true, or happens to be the accepted public policy. Furthermore, the object of persuasion is to persuade, that is, to induce conviction. As the first of our prohibitions, if scrupulously obeyed, would reduce democracy to a scientific laboratory, observance of the second would reduce it to a debating society. In either case, a democracy would lose its moral unity, which depends on devotion to a common creed.

❁   ❁   ❁

If we are to understand the right and wrong of propaganda *in a democracy,* we must turn to that creed itself and ask ourselves what limits that creed imposes on us. We must, in our propaganda *for* democracy, avoid if possible offending *against* democracy. If democracy consists essentially in the promotion of freedom and enlightenment out of respect for man, then our propaganda, if we are to do it with a good democratic conscience, must deliver men from bondage and ignorance, and promote their humanity.

We are committed to the idea that men shall live under a government of their own choosing. When we say "choosing" we mean free and enlightened choosing. It is not our idea that men's choice of their government shall be forced upon them by that government. Once a government exists, it exerts power and uses that power to penalize disobedience; but the democratic idea is that the very power which government possesses to exercise compulsion should be freely granted by those upon whom the compulsion is imposed. It is equally important, according to this democratic idea, that in choosing their government the people should know what they are choosing. They should know the range of possibilities from which they choose, and they should know the effects and

implications of these possibilities. Choice is
not enlightened if the people are kept in ignorance, or confused by passion, or narrowed
by habit. Choice is not enlightened if the
facts are falsified so that the consequences of
their choice are the opposite of what the
choosers have been led to expect.

Putting these two maxims together, the
fundamental assumption which explains our
democratic scruple against propaganda is
this: that the government and its policies
shall be the free and enlightened choice of
those who live under them; and that in order
to bring this about the government must make
and keep the people fully informed on the
matters related to their choice. Government
must not play upon fear or ignorance in secur-
ing its popular support. It must not create
fear and ignorance, whether by acts of com-
mission or by acts of omission; because in so
doing it is not really appealing to the choice
of its people, but is dictating that choice. It
is really choosing itself, and using its power
to entrench itself in power. It must not only
avoid intimidation and obscurantism: it must

actively encourage its people to choose freely, and facilitate such freedom, even though
their choice should result in its own rejec-
tion; and it must promote enlightenment,
even though as a result of that enlightenment
it should itself appear in an unfavorable
light. A government which obtains the re-
luctant assent of its people through their
fears, or the blind assent of its people through
their ignorance, whether this fear and this
ignorance result from artful demagoguery or
from neglect, is precisely what we mean by
the opposite of democracy—namely, tyranny.

If a society is to be democratic its members
must be not only free and enlightened, but
humane. They must desire the freedom and
enlightenment of others. Their love must be
deeper than their hate. They must be moved
by sympathy to feel for their fellow men, each
placing himself where the other stands and
sharing the other's needs, desires, and aspirations. Their choice will then be a choice not
in their own narrow behalf, but in behalf of
the total group or aggregate mankind to
which they belong.

❊   ❊   ❊

In the light of these considerations, let us now examine a statement of German propaganda, which will immediately evoke our democratic disapproval as it did that of the German liberal who wrote it. Up to the time of Hitler's ascendancy, the Director of the Museum of Ethnology in Cologne was Jules Lips, now in exile in America. His wife describes the effort of the Burgomaster, Herr Ebel, to convert the Museum into an agency of propaganda:

"Science? According to Herr Ebel and his party doctrine, that was the urge to supply a show of logic as a foundation for insane notions. A museum? An institute of propaganda for race theories spawned in the addled brains of eccentrics. A university professor? A nodding image, controlled by orders from above. A museum director? Advertising agent for the Third Reich. A lecture? Whatever the subject, a dissertation on the supremacy of the white race over the colored or the Jewish. . . . There was no longer a museum; there was no longer a University. There were only institutions of propaganda, brothels of the spirit. There were no longer any independent scholars — only tools of the new system. The walls of learning parted, and I saw the horrors behind them: soldiers, bayonets, falsehood and force. . . . Barbarians governed us, ordering us to become barbarians. Armed men gave orders, and their orders were to shoot. A muzzled dog on an iron chain; this was the spirit permitted and encouraged by the Third Reich." [4]

Here is propaganda in its essential evil, as judged by the standard of democracy. Why evil? Not because it is emotional. The author's righteous indignation is emotional, and we do not take exception to that. Our own response is emotional, and we can scarcely take exception to that. Not because Hitler and his agents proposed to indoctrinate the German people: the cult of science, the destruction of which both the author and the reader deplore, was in Germany and elsewhere the product of generations of indoc-

[4] Eva Lips, *Savage Symphony, A Personal Record of the Third Reich*, Random House, 1938, pp. 40–44. Quoted by permission of the publishers.

trination. No, the evil of this evil propaganda lay in its offense against humanity. It was abhorrent because it lied, intimidated, and brutalized, thereby depriving the German people of their power of free, enlightened, and kindly choice.

In the propaganda of Frau Lips herself, as distinguished from that which she describes and condemns, we see the positive side of these same considerations. It is not merely excusable propaganda, in that it avoids the evils of that propaganda which she exposes — it is good propaganda. It enlightens us concerning the nature of nazi methods, enables us freely to choose between the nazi way of life and our own, and warms our sympathies with the Hitler victims. Its deeper effect is to make us love more passionately than before the free, enlightened, and humane form of life. And it is effective propaganda. Its effect is attained by an artful appeal to our emotions. A statistical chart or "scientific" analysis of the nazi mind would have produced no such effect. *Savage Symphony* illustrates the fact that propaganda not only may but must excite and indoctrinate within the limits set by democratic standards. Choice must be free, enlightened, and humane; men must, however, be persuaded to *choose*, and to give themselves with full commitment and passionate devotion to the object of their choice.

To some it may seem that the opposite creed — of servitude, ignorance, and inhumanity, should receive a similar support and be given a similar hearing. It may be argued that every propaganda, democratic propaganda included, should be accompanied by an anti-propaganda. But why? To what end? Shall servitude be praised in order to make men free? Shall ignorance be praised in order to make men enlightened? And inhumanity in order that every human interest and attitude may obtain its due?

We are here confronted by the fundamental logic of the matter. The standard by which we judge the good and evil of propaganda itself stands outside the limits which that standard imposes on propaganda. If we advocate anti-democratic propaganda on

democratic grounds, then we contradict ourselves. I am fully aware that there may be
democratic reasons against suppressing anti-
democratic propaganda by the use of force,
lest the instruments of repression be abused.
I am also aware that an effective democratic
propaganda may embrace the statement and
the refutation of the opposite side. But if we
allow men to be exposed to anti-democratic
propaganda because it is more democratic so
to do, then our deeper desire must be that
men shall be imbued with a love of democracy — that is, of freedom, enlightenment,
and humanity. If men were hopelessly in-
fected with democracy from birth, we could
only rejoice.

*   *   *

This question has a wider scope than is
ordinarily recognized. We sometimes speak
as though propaganda were a special weapon,
like the gas-mask or the anti-aircraft gun,
which may be dispensed with in normal
times. We tend to the same view of morale.
Because propaganda and morale are pecul-

iarly necessary in times of crisis, we forget
that they are always necessary. They are the
conditions of social vigor, and when social
vigor is severely tested we then recognize its
conditions — as though discovering them for
the first time.

This misconception is partly due to words.
The words "propaganda" and "morale" become current in time of war, and we natu-
rally suppose that the things themselves have
just come into being. If for the word "propaganda" we substitute "moral education," and
if for the word "morale" we substitute "moral
unity," then we can see that their role in a
democracy is continuous, and no less important in times of peace. In fact, if they did not
exist in peace, they could not possibly be
effective in war. The stress of war can do
little more than awaken and redirect what is
already there, whether in the form of inher-
ited instincts or of acquired beliefs. Men do
not suddenly become democratic on the field
of battle. If they are not already so disposed
as a result of their whole previous history, it
will be too late. War propaganda can only

supplement the propaganda of every day. If the dispositions are not already there, the emergency will only disclose their absence: as, when a man is sound of limb, an unusual exertion will strengthen him; while when he is unsound, it will only break him down.

Propaganda is the activity which creates morale: or, moral education is the activity which creates moral unity. Without moral unity a society cannot, it is true, defend itself; but neither can it do business, develop a culture, or enjoy happiness. If men are to work together, play together, act together, live together they must be bound together by certain deeply rooted common attitudes. This is their moral unity — in a democracy, their democratic unity.

If this is to be, an incessant stream of influences must proceed from one individual to another and from each generation to the next. They must be all-pervasive, and mould the individual from his earliest childhood. The aggregate of these influences is moral education. The school or college is only one agency through which they are exerted. Every man who exhorts, criticizes, or praises his fellow men, or gives open expression to his judgments of good and evil — every parent, public speaker, writer, friend, and neighbor — is engaged in this activity.

As a matter of fact, the school and college, by a self-denying ordinance, endeavor to refrain from moral education, or leave it to the unregulated and extra-curricular influences of the community. They endeavor to confine themselves to instruction, and pride themselves on imparting only facts. They suffer the same disadvantage as a propaganda agency in a democracy. They are afraid to practice moral education openly and methodically; they know that it cannot be prevented; they do it with their left hands, or merely allow it to happen; and the result is that it is done badly.

The scruples of the teacher in a democracy are the same as those of a propagandist: he is afraid of indoctrination and of emotional appeal. But his fears are misdirected and his scruples are confused. He should be afraid of only three things: of deceiving his students or leaving them in ignorance; of

forcing beliefs upon them by intimidation;
and of stimulating their selfish appetites and
hardening their hearts. If he is motivated by
an honest desire to make his students enlightened, free, and humane, and if his methods are skillfully adapted to this end, he need
not and should not fear anything else. He
may be as eloquent as he pleases; he may
take full advantage of the innocence of
youth; he may touch the feelings of his students, excite their emotions, and form their
wills; provided only that the result is to en-
hance their capacity to choose for themselves
with a full knowledge of the facts, and with
a warm sympathy for their fellow men.

*   *   *

A democracy should enjoy the highest
morale, because its cause is the best cause.
But it can enjoy that advantage only by earn-
ing it. It must be strong in its own way,
through being true to its own peculiar genius.
We need that strength today, and we need
it most desperately. We have need of all of
our reserves — physical, mental, and moral.
For today we are called upon to meet an

altogether new test. Can a peace-loving democracy such as ours meet a league of great military dictatorships armed by the latest technology, aroused by the most primitive instincts, and bent on universal conquest? Though we can equal and surpass their science, we cannot, like them, wholly divest ourselves of civilization and conscience. We cannot be lashed into unreasoning fury — I have no words with which to do that, and I would not use them if I had. But we *can* prove that a love of the good can be as quick and as brave in the hour of danger as the greed for power and the lust for blood.

Hitherto we have been saved by the grace of God, who has given us distance and natural resources. If God is to save us now, he must do so through the force of our own moral wills. Now we can survive, if we are to survive, only by a bold and constructive leadership, loyally supported by an inspired people. Our blood stream must flow between our viscera and our higher centers, so that we can act and feel at the same time that our minds are dedicated to truth and to right.

CHAPTER IV

NAZI IDEOLOGY

Even five-syllable words can get themselves into the newspapers and into daily speech. One of the words that has recently been added to the English language is the word "ideology." As often happens, although the word is new, the thing itself is old.

Before discussing nazi ideology I want to say something about ideology in general. People can go to war without an ideology. They can go to war for power, or territory, or plunder; or they can go to war, as individuals can, simply because they have quarrelled and come to hate one another. But since the beginning of time people have gone to war on account of their beliefs. The oldest and most common form of this is religious war. When Christians fought Mohammedans, and protestants fought catholics, and puritan protestants fought anglican protestants, each side was held together by a religious creed. When people ceased to fight about religion they still found other ideas to fight for. In our Civil War, people fought for and against slavery; in the wars following the French Revolution people fought for Liberty, Equality and Fraternity against absolute monarchy.

Modern nationalism has encouraged this tendency. For a nation is not a geographical area, or a pure race, or a society living under one government, but a people bound together by a common tradition and "way of life" to which they are profoundly attached.

So when we speak of the nazi ideology, and of the opposing democratic ideology, we are speaking of what is only the newest form of a kind of rivalry and opposition of ideas in which history abounds.

An ideology, then, is an idea, or set of ideas, for which people live, and are willing if need be to fight. If they are willing to fight for an idea they must feel it to be important; and they must share it, or hold it in common. This does not mean that all of the people are conscious of the idea all the time, or that it furnishes the only motive for which they fight. But it will be in the minds of the more thoughtful people in their more thoughtful moments, and it will be appealed to as the deeper justification of the more immediate motives. It is certain, for example, that the Mohammedans who fought the Christians were not all good Mohammedans, or that everything they did was done for Mohammedan reasons; but when they wished to put their action on the highest ground, and have the support of conscience and reason, and create among themselves the greatest collective unity and enthusiasm, then they invoked their Mohammedan faith. So it is with the nazis and their faith; and so it is with us and our faith.

One more point about ideology in general before turning to the nazi ideology in particular. An ideology cannot be invented overnight. It must be in the line of tradition, and associated with illustrious names in the nation's past. Our own democratic ideology is traditionally American. It received a memorable statement in the American Declaration of Independence, and has been known for generations to "every American school boy." It is associated with the great names of Washington, Jefferson, and Lincoln. It is expressed in words, such as "freedom," "equality," "opportunity," "tolerance," and "government of the people," which will immediately excite applause in any not-too-sophisticated American audience to which they are addressed. Similarly the nazi ideology serves its purpose only because it is deeply rooted in the German past. It is possible to quote great Germans in its support, and it employs words such as *Volk, Geist,* and *Kultur,* which are peculiarly sweet to German ears.

*   *   *

While it is impossible that the nazi ideology should mean to Americans all that it means to Germans, there is nevertheless a simple way for Americans to understand this ideology — though it may still seem to them incredible that any one should believe it. For it happens that in essentials the nazi creed is almost the precise opposite of our own. Therefore we have only to think of our own, and then to think, point for point, of that which is most unlike it.

Our own ideology is composed of three main historic strands — the ancient Greco-Roman or Latin, the Hebraic-Christian, and the liberal. From the Greeks and Romans we have learned to think of culture as something universal or cosmopolitan, belonging to all mankind, expressing the highest human faculties, and dedicated to the paramount ideals of truth, beauty, goodness, and law. From Hebraism and Christianity we have learned to think that the highest of the virtues, the greatest of the commandments, is love — love of God and love of neighbor. From modern liberalism we have learned to think of mankind in terms of individual men and women, each with a claim or right to happiness and self-development, and to the control of his own destinies within limits set by the similar rights of others.

While these three strands have a certain degree of independence they are historically interwoven. The individualism of the Greeks and Romans was developed by Christianity into a respect for the sacredness of the human soul or personality. In the great civilization of the Middle Ages, Christianity was blended with the pagan idea of universal culture, and the Christian trinity of virtues — faith, hope and love — took their place beside the ancient virtues of temperance, justice, courage, and wisdom. Modern liberalism took over the humanitarian ideal of Christianity and the humanistic ideal of paganism, and taught us that they depend on freedom, tolerance, and equal opportunity of personal development. So there has grown up in Europe and America an ideology composed of these three elements, in which each is not merely added to the others but has enriched and to some extent transformed them. This is that moral ideology of which our Americanism is a special form — with a peculiar local coloring of its own, but shared in its essentials with a large part of the modern world.

The opposite ideology, then, would be anti-

Latin, anti-Christian, and anti-liberal. And these are precisely what the nazi ideology is. These are not terms of abuse employed by its enemies, but what nazism means to be, and is proud of being. Germany has felt all of the three impulses which I have named and has contributed richly to their unfolding. The culture of Greco-Roman antiquity, Christianity both catholic and protestant, and modern liberalism, have entered deeply into the life of Germany and have found among Germans many of their greatest exponents. It would be false to history to deny this or even question it. Nevertheless it is true that in no other European country have Latin, Christian and liberal influences been so consistently escaped or resisted and their opposites so frequently and continuously affirmed.

*   *   *

Let us now ask ourselves just what in German terms this anti-Latin, anti-Christian, anti-liberal ideology means.

In the first place, it substitutes for a universal or cosmopolitan culture, a culture of the German race. For a universal religion it substitutes a Germanic religion, worshiping a tribal God, or deifying the soul of the tribe itself. In every branch of culture the same tribal standard is applied. The best art and music is the most German art and music. The artist or composer does not try to rise above his own breed and locality and feel his kinship with the best art and music of all ages and peoples, but becomes as German as possible and then lets himself go. The best literature is that which deals with German themes in the German manner. The scientist conceives even of truth as German. He takes the fantastic view that the best physics or mathematics is a German physics or mathematics, in which the peculiar mentality of the tribe is substituted for that evidence of sense and reason which is the same for all men, and which unites the scientists of all nations in the creation of a common body of knowledge.

More serious still, because it leads more directly to action, is the tribal standard of good and right. Instead of a conscience of mankind, or a universal code of justice, veracity, happiness, and human perfection, this ideology adopts a Germanic code, recognizing only one moral obligation — the obligation, namely, to exalt the power of Germany. This code binds a man to his fellow Germans, but as between Germans and the rest of the world it recognizes no moral relations whatever.

*　　　　*　　　　*

In the second place, the nazi ideology rejects the Christian teaching of love. What does it substitute? What is the opposite of love? The answer is clear. Love pities and gives — its essence is sympathy. It enters into the feelings of others, seeks their happiness, and shrinks from inflicting pain. The enemies of Christianity have understood this and have attacked Christianity as a code of weakness, because it has taught man to be self-denying and compassionate. The opposite, then, of the Christian code of love is the code of physical strength, power, force, and the admiration of all those traits which make for force, such as self-assertion, animal vigor, hardness, ruthlessness and discipline.

*   *   *

Finally, what does anti-liberalism mean? If liberalism is essentially a belief in individual rights, anti-liberalism is the denial of these rights. And what is put in their place?

The opposite of the individual is not another individual, or a multitude of individuals, but another kind of thing altogether. It is a collective or social thing, such as a family, a corporation, a nation, or a state. The opposite of individualism, then, is to exalt this social thing at the expense of its individual members. Men and women are not beings in themselves, but are merely parts, like the cells of a physical organism; and the social thing is the end, of which the individual members are merely the means and instruments. Toward this entity the members have duties; against this entity they have no rights.

To us, bred in another tradition, it is as though this social thing were a sort of

Moloch appeased by human sacrifices, or one of those monsters that devour their own children. But we can understand the view more sympathetically when we think in terms of the motives of blind loyalty and obedience by which individuals willingly surrender themselves to the larger whole to which they belong and allow that whole to use them and speak for them. These motives are primitive and lasting, and can easily be aroused.

In practice, anti-individualism turns into the tyranny of one individual. The reason is that the social thing has no organs of its own — no hands and feet, no viscera, no heart, no mouth, no brain. If it is to think and act, *some* individual has to think and act for it. But what individual is *entitled* to think and act for it? This cannot be decided by a vote of the individual members of the group, each acting in the light of his own interest and intelligence; for according to the anti-individualistic theory the ruler is not supposed to represent any individual, or even a majority of individuals, but a very different thing, namely, the organic whole. Theoretically the ruler should be he who expresses the mind of that whole — the soul of Germany, for example. But since the whole has no way of telling who this privileged individual is, he has to designate himself, and *claim* to speak for the whole. There are always individuals who are willing to do this: the father to speak for the family, the director to speak for the corporation, or the dictator to speak for the nation or state. The theory thus serves to justify any ruler or any self-appointed Führer who pretends to be the inspired voice of the social entity — and can get away with it.

❋   ❋   ❋

These opposite ideas, like the Greco-Roman idea of universal culture, the Christian idea of love, and the liberal idea of individualism, also form a consistent pattern. They compose the ideology which teaches that there is a higher social being, such as the German race, which substitutes its own private *Kultur* for the universal standards of beauty, truth, goodness, and legality; which dedicates itself to its own power regardless of the balance of mankind; and which imposes its will on its own members and on the balance of mankind under its inspired dictator.

This doctrine is plainly set forth in Hitler's *Mein Kampf*, in which it is clear that he takes himself to be the inspired dictator, whom he describes as that "one man" who must "step forward in order to form . . . granite principles, and take up the fight for their sole correctness, until out of the playing waves of a free world of thought a brazen sort of uniform combination of will and form arises." Elsewhere he says, of his "folkish state," that it recognizes "the obligation in accordance with the Eternal Will that dominates this universe to promote the victory of the better and stronger, and to demand the submission of the worse and the weaker." Such a state, he continues, "cannot grant the right of existence to an ethical idea if this idea represents a danger for the racial life of the bearers of the higher ethics." And he concludes, finally, that "we all sense in the distant future problems . . . for the conquest of which only a highest race, as a master-nation, based upon the means and the possibilities of an entire globe, will be called upon." [1]

This ideology is directly, expressly, and dangerously opposed to the cause for which the United Nations fight today. It teaches war, and it teaches conquest. What "distant future" Hitler had in mind when he spoke of global domination by a master-race we do not know. But we do know that his master-nation is Germany. We know that Hitler claims the right to decide the time. And there is reason to believe that the time is now.

The ideas which compose this nazi ideology were not invented by Hitler, and did not arise as a result of the First World War and the Treaty of Versailles. They find high sanction in the historic past of Germany. If Hitler himself did not originally know this, Rosenberg and others did, and taught him. By going over the German past, selecting what

[1] *Mein Kampf*, Reynal and Hitchcock, 1939, pp. 577–81.

fits and rejecting the rest, it is possible to trace this ideology in an almost continuous thread from legendary Nibelungen days, through the Teutonic knights and the early history of Prussia, through the uprising against Napoleon, and through the building of the Hohenzollern Empire, to the humiliation of 1918 and the growth of the nazi power. It is possible, sometimes by omission and distortion, but sometimes by citing them truthfully and in full, to claim for this ideology the support of reformers, statesmen, historians, philosophers, and poets — Martin Luther, Frederick the Great, Fichte, Hegel, Trietschke, Mommsen, Wagner, Nietzsche, and a host of lesser men whose names are names to conjure with in Germany.

❋   ❋   ❋

Germany has also her roll of honor — her great mediaeval emperors, her humanists, her Kant of the Age of the Enlightenment, her Goethe and Lessing of the early nineteenth century, her exemplars of Christian piety, catholic and protestant, and the successive generations of liberals who have suffered exile and martyrdom in her repeated and unsuccessful struggles for political freedom. No critics of the German ideology have been more severe than those Germans who in anguish of soul and with a sense of helplessness have spoken out against their own fatal inheritance.

Friedrich William Foerster is one of those who have identified this evil creed with the spirit of Prussia:

"And so this powerful race of Prussian conquerors had of necessity to become a tragic curse to itself and to the world, just because every capacity for moral conquest, every spark of understanding of others' natures or endeavors was lost in its harsh, stern manner, in its certainty that it could not be surpassed. . . . In it was already the dreadful doom that it did not serve God, nor even a supreme ethical idea; but it served the state, and the logic of the state was raised on principle above the moral law. . . . A man in the civil administration of Belgium . . . defined for me the essence of all recent German activity . . . : 'A highly developed organization in the service of moral anarchy!' " [2]

The poet Fritz von Unruh, addressing himself to those who like himself had had their eyes opened at the time of the First World War, finds the root of the evil in the German's lack of individual self-reliance:

"To fall back into guilt, after the clatter of death in a brother's bones once went to our very marrow: that means being damned in the eyes of future ages. . . . There they go, those who are willing to bow their necks again to Mammon and the Kaiser; those who long for their true home as the slave longs for the lash, and would rather do anything than accept responsibility.

But you, whose hearts beat high, — there you sit and wait, wait for a miracle to happen, and look outside and listen to the noise hoping to hear a *voice* — ?

And for eons you have not heard the cry of pain of the man who lies captive deep within

[2] *Mein Kampf gegen das militaristische und nationalistische Deutschland*, 1920, tr. by Evan B. Davis, quoted by Will Schaber, in *Thinker vs. Junker*, 1941, pp. 223–226.

your heart — the man who waits within you all — waits not for the *One*, the *Master*, but — *for you!*" [3]

There is, then, another Germany which would, if it could, fight beside the United Nations in this struggle. Whether that other Germany shall triumph at home and enable the German people to take their place with the United Nations in a free world where all nations shall enjoy security and fruitful intercourse hangs on the issue of present events. With the nazi ideology, and with the men whose deeds it is now used to justify, there can be no compromise.

* * *

By an extraordinary and most ominous coincidence, at the very time that this German ideology is bearing its practical fruits in nazism, a parallel ideology is springing into action on the opposite side of the globe. In its modern technology, industrial and military, Japan has been imitative, but its ideology is

[3] *Vaterland und Freiheit,* 1923; quoted by Will Schaber, *op. cit.,* pp. 243–44.

as original as its German counterpart, and of a purer type. Its statism is symbolized by the worship of the Emperor, its militarism is rooted in the cult of the Samurai, and its expanding nationalism in the belief that the race of Nippon are the chosen of the gods. As the arrogance of the Germans has been heightened and embittered by a sense of inferiority to the peoples of western and southern Europe, so the Japanese have suffered from a sense of their cultural dependence on the ancient empire of China. In Germany this ideology has been resisted and tempered by Christianity and liberalism, in Japan it has had a freer scope.[4]

Germany and Japan are partners in the spirit as well as allies in war. Both nations possess the same capacity to infuse the primitive instincts with a mystical faith and with artful mendacity; and to implement them with the most advanced techniques of science. Both nations, despite their distance

[4] Cf. Edwin O. Reischauer, "Wherein Are We Challenged: Japan," *Christian Science Monitor*, June 27, 1942.

and their independent origin, have been inoculated with the same creed: the subordination of the individual man to the state; the docile and disciplined acceptance of authority; the inhumane and unscrupulous cult of force; the destiny of a master race to conquer and enslave.

There is no hope for mankind in the prediction that these rival claimants for world domination will some day destroy one another, for before that day they intend to divide the world between them. Before that last war between the triumphant forces of evil they will have cleared the field. The time to meet them is now, when free nations pledged to the opposite faith can still subdue them both.

CHAPTER V

A BRIDGE TO RUSSIA

W HEN Germany invaded Russia on June 22, 1941, Russia became the major enemy of our major enemy. After having for two years played the role of Germany's friendly neutral, she was suddenly "on our side"; and when, after December 7, we ourselves entered the war she became by force of circumstance our military ally. The magnificent and unexpected fighting qualities of the Russian armies and the unity, endurance, and spirit of the Russian people excited our admiration. Immediately exposed to the full strength of the German military power along a frontier of more than two thousand miles, Russia became the chief combatant among the allies and offered the best hope of a swift and decisive victory.

Almost overnight the current of American feeling was reversed. Russia became heroic,

the slogan "Aid to Russia" took its place beside "Aid to Britain," while "Russian War Re-
lief" superseded "Bundles for Britain" as the
fashionable charity. The word "Red" ceased
to be a signal of alarm; Stalin's stature increased, and he lost his tail and cloven hoofs;
agents of the Soviet government were wel-
comed in Washington in exchange for Harry
Hopkins. And through the Anglo-Soviet
Treaty of May 26, 1942, and the diplomatic
exchanges between Washington and Moscow, Russia has now become an equal part-
ner with Britain and the United States,
pledged to the same objectives and to the
sharing of whatever costs and labors may be
necessary for the overthrow of the Axis powers. As adherent of the Atlantic Charter, and
as maker and guardian of the peace to come,
Russia has solemnly assumed with the other
United Nations a joint responsibility for that
future freedom and security on which the
peoples of the world have fixed their hearts
and hopes.

These events have occurred with breath-
taking rapidity, precipitated by the threat of

a common enemy and by the belligerent and patriotic emotions which that threat has excited. It now behooves us to strengthen the intellectual and moral foundations of this union and to create a unified strategy of peace as well as of war. While it is immediately imperative that military resources should be pooled and military action coördinated, it is also and at the same time necessary that long-range purposes should be shared, and common principles found on which to work together for a lasting cure of the present grave disorders which have all but destroyed the elaborate and delicate fabric of civilization.

To suppose that this task can be performed by partners who are merely polite to one another — having patched up a temporary truce in the presence of a common danger, while reserving their old hostilities and suspicions for a more convenient occasion — is not only foolish but in the highest degree dangerous. An alliance with enemy number two *until enemy number one shall be disposed of,* assumes a future time when number two will become number one. It anticipates a new war while waging this. Even a military alliance on such a basis is precarious and ineffective. It is impossible to give undivided attention to the present enemy if one must at the same time guard one's flanks against one's own ally. The time will come to make peace with those who are now our enemies: we must begin by making peace with our friends.

Let us, therefore, frankly recognize the causes which have divided us from our Russian ally and make every effort to remove them. Momentarily forgotten in the heat of action and in the presence of overwhelming danger there remain old suspicions and slumbering enmities. To remove them it is not necessary to blot out the past or shut our eyes to facts. That again would be dangerous, for neither the past nor the facts will cease to exist merely through being ignored. It is not necessary to repudiate either conscience or conviction. If we have hated the cruelties of the Bolshevik Revolution and of its later liquidations and purges, if we have con-

demned the debasing practices of terrorism,
if we have believed that the Russo-German
Pact let loose the present war and that the
attack on Finland was an unjustifiable aggression, if we have disapproved the hostility to religion and rejected the Marxist
economy, there is no reason for reversing
these judgments. It would be childish and
shallow to rush now to the opposite extreme,
and proclaim the infallibility of Soviet policy
or identify communist Russia with Utopia.

The cure lies not in the substitution of an
opposite partisan emotion, but in magnanimity and understanding. To be fair towards
those whom circumstances have made our
allies is both necessary and permissible, and
involves no recantation or disloyalty. Thus,
for example, to remind ourselves of the evils
of Czarist Russia will automatically moderate
our judgment of the excesses of the Revolution and create a base line by which to measure its failures and successes. Or, to become
more vividly aware of the failures of our own
democracy — our failure to prevent the great
depression of 1930, or to solve the problems

of unemployment, poverty and racial dis-
crimination — will make us more tolerant of
those who are attempting to solve these problems in other ways.

❈   ❈   ❈

Similarly, it is a wholesome exercise to re-
view the events of the last ten years in the
aspect which they presented to Russia.
Hitler, soon after his accession to power, at-
tempted with considerable success to organize a world-wide offensive against communism as a cover for his territorial designs
upon the Ukraine. Whereupon Russia, threatened on both her Eastern and Western frontiers, turned away from her policy of world-
revolution and sought pacts and alliances
with the western powers. She participated
in the Disarmament Conference at Geneva,
joined the League of Nations, and played an
active part in the Non-Intervention Commit-
tee in London. If Russia's diplomatic repre-
sentatives during this period were not always
popular among their associates it was often
because they took the principle of collective

security too seriously. They called a spade a spade — and frequently alluded to spades. Even those Americans who adhere to a pro-Franco view of the Spanish Civil war will at least credit the Russians with having seen that Axis intervention *was* intervention; and in the light of subsequent events Russians will be pardoned for thinking that the victory of Franco was a victory for the Axis, and that through their failure to support the Spanish Loyalists the now United Nations lost a key to the Mediterranean.

The Munich crisis of 1938–1939 found Russia ready to stand by her engagements and face the consequences. If the word "appeasement" was, even in America, a byword for timidity, vacillation, and shortsightedness, it is not surprising that the Chamberlain policy should have created a profound and bitter disillusionment in Russia. To a nation threatened with invasion, the failure of England and France to maintain a bold and united front against Hitler was something more than a joke about an umbrella. In all fairness it is not surprising that under the circumstances

Russia should have tried a little appeasing on her own account. If it was natural that the western powers, at long last committed to war against Hitler, should have resented the Russo-German pact of 1939, it was also natural that Russia's distrust of the western powers should by that time have become too deep to permit her only a few months after Munich to assume all the immediate military risks of defending a Poland into which she was not even permitted to send her armies.

*   *   *

But the heart of the matter is our relation to communism itself. It is sometimes said that Russia has renounced communism and reverted to nationalism. That the present struggle has drawn upon the older and deeper reserves of Russian patriotism and blurred the lines between "Red" and "White" is no doubt true. But it would be foolish and dangerous to count upon the adoption of a capitalistic democracy in Russia. It appears probable that the present unity of Russia is largely the result of the communist faith;

and that the war will confirm that faith in the sentiment and conviction of the Russian people. If we are to avoid wishful thinking and avert a revival of old antipathies we must prepare our minds to come to an understanding not with a Russia refashioned on our own model, but with a communist Russia. That is the other pier on which we must build our bridge of mutual understanding and coöperation. It is not impossible that we may someday have to build a similar bridge to a communist China.

Nor will it do to count upon Russian isolationism. It is no doubt true that Russia, having failed to revolutionize the rest of the world, would have liked to retire behind impregnable barriers and devote her energies and resources to the development of her own internal economy. But this policy has already lost its meaning. In the world of modern technology distance and barriers are as obsolete for Russia as for the United States. Russia is playing and will continue to play a leading role in the family of nations — with ourselves. We shall encounter Russia in every part of the world. With Russia certainly, and with a communist Russia probably, we must learn to live and to coöperate for an indefinite future.

The heart of communism is a collectivist economy in which the social benefits of production are sought directly by public control rather than indirectly by private ownership, competition, and the profit motive. Russian communism and American regulated capitalism both justify themselves by the same standard, namely, the maximum satisfaction of human needs and wants by inventive enterprise and widening distribution. Both systems profess the same desire to raise the level of the masses of the people and to get rid not only of poverty, disease, and ignorance, but of unfairness, parasitic privilege, and wage slavery. Both seek the freedom of the individual, while differing in the tyrannies they fear.

Communists believe that the chief enemy of freedom is the unofficial tyranny of private wealth, masked by the forms of democracy; capitalists believe that the chief enemy of freedom is the official tyranny of centralized government. Communists believe that as capitalism evolves it ceases to yield the social benefits which its adherents claim for it; and that in the long run it breaks down altogether, because its productive capacity outruns consumers' purchasing power. Capitalists, on the other hand, believe that communism is unworkable because of its elaborate bureaucratic mechanisms and its violations of human nature. Communists point out that capitalistic countries are finding it more and more necessary to resort to collectivistic remedies; while capitalists point out that communism has found it necessary to preserve or restore the practices of capitalism.

All of these differences are arguable in terms of the same general objective and in the light of experience. Communistic and capitalistic societies can engage in peaceful intercourse across national frontiers. Or a solution may be found in different combinations of the two methods, suited to the peculiar habits and conditions of particular countries. Both systems are opposed to the static acceptance of a primitive economy, and to an otherworldly indifference to human suffering and privation; both are opposed to a Spartan or Prussian military cult of self-imposed hardship, and to the exploitation of enslaved masses by a master-class or of enslaved nations by a master-race.

*   *   *

The remaining grounds of objection to communism on the part of Americans have to do with its attacks on the family, the state, and the church. The first step towards understanding is to observe that in the communist doctrine all of these institutions are conceived in economic terms. The whole point of the attack lies there.

The family, for example, is conceived not in terms of love and fidelity, or in terms of the procreation and care of the young, but in terms of the capitalistic system. A family in which the father has ceased to exploit his wife and children, or in which domestic life is no longer degraded by poverty and grinding labor, has, from the communist point of view, ceased to be a "family." The institution, in other words, is named for the economic evils of which it is symptomatic. In capitalistic countries, on the other hand, the family represents certain moral values and social functions which are no less esteemed in communism, but which according to that doctrine can be realized only by a changed economy. For the ideas which revolt the American conscience — the debasing of the woman to the role of household servant and child-bearer, the encouragement of extra-marital relations for the augmentation of population, and the training of the child from early years for the uses of the state — one must look not to communism but to nazism.

The state, conceived in terms of the communist political philosophy, is an institution designed to protect the interest of a special economic class, the owners, namely, of private capital. The state being so conceived, the success of communism implies its overthrow, and the creation, after a period of proletarian dictatorship, of a society which is both classless and stateless. In other words,

the state which is to be overthrown by revolution, or is to "wither away" through having
no longer any function in a socialist society,
is an abstraction that has never existed except
in Marxist dogma. Some sort of central administration and coercion exercised by organized society is inescapable. The Stalin Constitution of 1936 provides for the equivalent
of a state, and it would not be improper to
describe it as a democracy. It is true that this
political program, like present Russian practice, will seem to Americans to place too little
emphasis on civil liberties; but if it is deficient
in this respect it is to be credited with a com-
pensatory emphasis on the individual's rights
to work, to rest, to medical care, and to education. If it is less libertarian it is more provi-
dent. In any case it rests fundamentally on
the suffrage of the people who live under it,
and who obey it freely because they see it to
be the instrument of their good.

If communists have erred in identifying
the actual state with its abuses, we, on our
side, have perhaps erred in identifying it
with what it professes to be. If both will dis-

tinguish between the ideal and the actual there is hope of an understanding. Any candid adherent of democracy will admit that in practice the state is deflected from its true purpose by a variety of influences, including the influence exerted by concentrated wealth. Similarly, a candid adherent of communism will admit that if and when the Stalin Constitution is carried into effect the Soviet state will likewise contain some admixture of impurity. The state is, and ever will be, a rough approximation to that perfect disinterestedness and devotion to the public good for which it is created.

That the government of Russia since the Revolution has been and remains a dictatorship, no one doubts. The revolutionary party which established itself by violence still rules by force. Many critics of communism doubt whether a completely collectivistic economy is consistent with democratic or even constitutional government. But I am here concerned with ideas and not with practices — with those ideas which it is reasonable to hope will someday be translated into practices. Judg-

ing communistic Russia by her political aspirations (as we claim the right to judge ourselves) it is possible to find an identity which
not only unites us with communistic Russia
but unites us against the political aspirations
of nazi Germany. For we are both profoundly
and unalterably opposed to the deification of
the state, to the absolute authority of an élite
or master-race, and to the absorption of the
individual into a monstrous corporate force.
With Russians, even communists, we can, if
we talk long enough, speak the same political language. From the political principles
of nazi Germans we are more profoundly
divided in the depths even than on the surface. We can only turn away at last with
incredulity and irreconcilable hostility.

*   *   *

In the case of religion, Marxism again
starts with an economic interpretation. Religion is either "the opiate of the poor," by
which the exploited are drugged into submission by their exploiters; or it is the church
conceived as an institution devoted to its own

vested interests and to the support of the propertied class. This Marxist view seemed to Russian revolutionaries, as it did to the French and Spanish revolutionaries, to be confirmed by their own experience. In any case, if religion is by definition a capitalistic instrument then the overthrow of capitalism implies its destruction. And if it is reasonable to ask men who have suffered from the abuses of religion to distinguish between the spiritual essence and the economic accident, it is also reasonable to ask the friends of religion candidly to admit that religion *is* sometimes supported by the rich because it reconciles the poor to their lot; and that the church as a human institution *has* acquired property and power, and has in some measure allowed these to compromise its piety.

Except in its own doctrinaire terms communism is not opposed to religion. It is not opposed to the Christian gospel, least of all to the social teachings of compassion and human dignity. For the moral core of Christianity, as well as for freedom of religion conceived as a form of culture, there is room within a communist as well as within a capitalist society.

There is nothing more remarkable in the history of human sentiment than the unprotesting acceptance by the conscience of Christendom of the harsher aspects of modern industrialism. I do not refer to mass poverty: Christianity *is* disturbed by that and seeks to alleviate it. I refer to the motivation of capitalism — self-interest, the desire for gain, competition, bargaining, taking advantage of another's helplessness. One can understand that Christians might recognize these motives as ineradicable and necessary while at the same time deploring them as a part of the sinful proclivity of the natural man. And this is, as a matter of fact, the view which Christianity took for many centuries, during which it fought against usury and a wage scale based wholly on the labor market. But now the conscience of Christians by and large — I do not say of all Christians — not only endorses the capitalistic motivation but selects for its severest condemnation the economic philosophy which seeks to alter it.

Hence the astounding paradox that while "anti-Christians" are trying to build a society founded on the creative and generous impulses and purged of covetousness and selfish gain, Christians charge them with taking too idealistic a view of human nature.

* * *

In judging communism and nazism from the standpoint of religion the surface appearances are favorable to nazism, and reflect the differences between the techniques of the two revolutions. Recognizing the strength of both the catholic and Lutheran confessions, Hitler has temporized. He has called himself a Christian, has negotiated compromises with the church authorities, and freely refers to "God" as the sanction of his policies. Communism, on the other hand, has made a bold frontal attack on religion, on Christianity, on the church, and on God. Like its attack on private property, its method has been more honest, but it has also been more violent and more brutal. As a consequence Hitler has been able, when it suited his policy, to proclaim himself with some plausibility the champion of religion as well as of property against the communist menace. German Christians, like German industrialists, living at close quarters, have learned to fear the champion more than the menace. It is time that Christians at a distance should learn the same lesson.

For nazism is profoundly and irreconcilably opposed to the Christian religion in its spiritual, and not merely in its ecclesiastical, sense. As totalitarianism it can tolerate no divided allegiance, and must possess itself of men's souls as well as of their bodies. Its racism is opposed to any universal faith or recognition of human brotherhood. Its distinction between the élite and the masses insults the dignity of man. Its statism explicitly rejects the irreducible reality and preciousness in the eyes of God of the individual human soul. Its militarism despises the gospel of love. This is nazi doctrine, and this is from all reports the private and personal attitude of Hitler himself. Rauschning records him (all too credibly) as having said:

"For our people it is decisive whether they acknowledge the Jewish Christ-creed with its effeminate pity-ethics, or a strong, heroic belief in God in Nature, God in our own people, in our destiny, in our blood. . . . One is either a German or a Christian. You cannot be both." [1]

An eminent catholic clergyman for whom I have great respect has referred to communism as "Caesarism," and to communism and nazism as the "twin offspring" of "paganism and rationalism." [2] That communism is opposed to Caesarism in its fundamental philosophy seems to me to need no further argument; but I would give much if I could persuade my catholic friends that communism is not the blood brother of nazism. That it has rationalist and pagan ancestry I would not deny, but its bloodstream also contains a rich strain of that championship of the oppressed against the oppressor which is one of the

[1] Hermann Rauschning, *Voice of Destruction*, 1940, p. 49. Quoted by permission of G. P. Putnam and Sons, publishers.
[2] Rev. Edmund J. Walsh, S.J., as quoted in the *Boston Herald* for April 26, 1942.

things that is meant by Christianity. It is this kinship, however distant and mixed with alien blood, that I beg all Christians to acknowledge.

❖   ❖   ❖

In a recent article on "Religion and Politics in France" Jacques Maritain quotes a public statement made by the Archbishop of Toulouse in June, 1941, on the eve of the German invasion of Russia:

"It is the future of the Christian spirit which is at stake in this hour — a future that may extend over centuries. Many priests, many Catholics, do not realize this. . . . Their mission is to save and to spread the Christian spirit. . . . Let us impregnate ourselves with the Gospels. Let us read St. Paul and tell ourselves that since the fall of the Roman Empire, Catholics have had no more beautiful or greater mission — the salvation of the world, not through clericalism, of which the Church disapproves and of which we want nothing at any price, but the salvation of the world through the Cross of Jesus Christ, the manifestation and the symbol of infinite love." [3]

A prayer which the Archbishop caused to be read in the Cathedral of Toulouse contained the following petition:

"Sacred Heart of Jesus, I beg of You, do not permit the chivalrous soul of France to become the prey of error, of evil deeds and of brutality. Do not permit that the dignity of the human person and the right which that person possesses from its Creator — that the dignity of the family, which is not merely a supplier of children — that the dignity of the Fatherland desired by God, which is not an idol — shall ever disappear from a world from which Your kingdom is banished." [4]

The Archbishop's meaning is unmistakable. He urges catholic Christians to distinguish between the Christian spirit and the institutional interest of the church. In times of violence and insecurity it is of the utmost

[3] "Religion and Politics in France," *Foreign Affairs*, vol. 20, no. 2 (January, 1942), p. 279. Quoted by permission of the publishers.
[4] *Loc. cit.*

importance to know the deadly enemy from the merely dangerous enemy. Russian anti-clericalism may be a danger to the church, but this is a danger that can be met in the future, as it has been in the past, by magnanimity and peaceful negotiation. For it is not directed against "the Christian spirit," but against what are thought to be the mistaken economic policies of the church. Christian communism is conceivable; Christians may approve or reject communism, and yet, in the deeper sense of the gospel, be Christians. Christian nazism, on the other hand, is a contradiction in terms.

*   *   *

The bridge between democratic United States and communist Russia must be built from both ends. On the communist side that which stands in the way is not its ultimate aspiration. "From each according to his ability; to each according to his needs" is both Christian and democratic as well as Marxist.[5] Communism, like democracy, describes

[5] *Handbook of Marxism*, edited by Emile Burns,

the good life of man in terms of peace, justice, fraternity, self-respect, and personal develop- ment. Its deeper impulse is profoundly hu- mane, and profoundly moral. But the com- munist mind suffers from the distortions of revolution, from historic grievances, and from an inheritance of rigid doctrinal or- thodoxy.

When communism is charged with at- tempting to destroy the family, the state, and the church, it does not reply by referring to its own domestic, political, and religious ideals. It resorts to polemical reprisals. It points out that these institutions are not what they pretend to be, and that the proletarian masses enjoy none of their promised benefits.[6] Thus the charges and the countercharges simply do not meet. Communists attack the abuses, and "bourgeois democrats" defend the uses. Each tends in its own way to be doctrinaire — communism to define the in- stitution by its abuses, democracy to define it

1935, p. 756. For other statements of the ideal end- result of the communist revolution, cf. *ibid.*, pp. 44, 46–47, 940.

[6] Cf. the famous *Communist Manifesto* of 1848.

by its uses. Hence the first seems to be attempting to destroy what the other would
keep, when they are really aiming at the same
goal. Except that the temper of communism
is revolutionary and that of democracy re-
formist, they agree as to what *are* the uses
and the abuses, and on the desirability of
perfecting the one and removing the other.

It is true that communism teaches moral
relativism and rejects the traditional morality, like the family, the state, and the church,
as a manifestation of bourgeois society. But
stripped of Marxian dogmas it comes to this.
So long as mankind is divided into warring
classes and nations the concrete details of its
morality and institutions will reflect this
rivalry of interests. To achieve universality it
is necessary to have an international and
classless society, and this can be accomplished
only by the overthrow of the predatory nation-state and the predatory capitalistic class.
But this is already a universal morality in its
broad outlines — a morality of justice, equality, humanity, and peace. And this morality
has emerged in the nation-state amidst its

warring classes! If this is so, then there is no reason why its implications should not be peacefully and coöperatively developed in all societies, whether communistic or democratic-capitalistic, which accept it as a standard.[7]

*   *   *

Soon after Russia took her place among the victims of nazi aggression Winston Churchill said, "Our fortunes are linked together." He was then thinking of the common danger and the need of a common resistance to that danger. It is already clear that there is a bond of opportunity, as well as a bond of necessity. To forfeit this opportunity through habits of fear and suspicion would be an unmitigated tragedy. To leave any means untried by which to forge an enduring moral bond out of the present linkage of our fortunes would be a grave disservice both to ourselves and to mankind. The possibilities of such a bond can be found in the deeper humane impulses of the Russian and

[7] Cf. Edmund Wilson's admirable *To the Finland Station*, 1940, pp. 197–198.

the Anglo-Saxon peoples. An American journalist reports that shortly after Munich a
member of the Japanese Diet predicted war
between Japan and Russia because, as he
said:

"The world is split into two camps, and it is
split on an ideological issue. Whether we like
it or not, we belong with Hitler. And whether
the Russians like it or not, they belong with
you. Russia belongs with the countries where
the little people still count." [8]

If we think of social progress in terms of
the lifting of all members of the human race
from bondage, from misery, and from barbarism to a plane on which they can lead the
life that becomes a man; if we consider the
brutality of man to man as a desecration of
human nature; if we are moved by compassion towards the unfortunate and by faith in
their potentialities; if we are resolved to develop the inventive and creative powers of
man to the utmost, and extend their benefits
to all; if we seek on every side and in every

[8] Ernest O. Hauser, "Siberia's Phony Peace," *Satur-
day Evening Post*, May 16, 1942, p. 62.

human relationship to substitute peace for war and coöperation for conflict; if we feel ourselves linked with every man in a common moral enterprise — if this is our side, then, I submit, Russia belongs with us, and we with Russia. And I submit that the best way by which to rid ourselves of the fears and suspicions that still divide us is to think positively in terms of the goal by which we are united.

CHAPTER VI

THE MORAL BASIS OF WORLD ORDER

Two months after Pearl Harbor a well-known column writer delivered himself as follows:

"Suspended for the duration, and if necessary by the neck, provided nothing less tender will shut their effort-drugging bazoos, should be those mighty minds who're always telling us what sort of peace we should have. It's nice of them to do the heavy thinking while somebody else does the heavy fighting. . . . They may mean all right, but they're chloroform held to the nose of a stripped down prize-fighter. They are sand on the axles and soap on the tracks. America's got to spit on its rapidly blistering hands. . . ." [1]

Despite my sneaking admiration for his command of the English language, I, one of

[1] *Boston Herald*, February 15, 1942.

his "effort-drugging bazoos," venture to dispute this writer's understanding of human nature. I doubted it at the time, and the experience of the last six months has converted my doubts into certainty. People are not divisible into sleep-walkers and prize-fighters. If you are to get the most out of any man you have to enlist the whole of him — his reason and his conscience as well as his viscera and blistering hands. To strip for action it is well to get rid of fat about the waist line, but no man or nation is slowed down by an excess of gray matter in the cranium. The fight which this writer is talking about, and which we are all agreed is the immediate duty of the moment, is not the blind fury of a berserker or one-eyed cyclops, but a sustained and directed effort with the goal in view and well-laid plans for its achievement.

What is the goal? The immediate goal is victory, but the ultimate goal is peace. To seek the second goal does not retard the attainment of the first because the way to the second lies through the first, and because the desire for the second strengthens the desire for the first. When, after Pearl Harbor, we engaged the enemy and no longer merely feared him, it seemed to many, such as the ferocious journalist quoted above, that our horizon would and should contract. Just the opposite has happened. Now that the war is today, post-war is tomorrow: the one actual, the other imminent. As men begin to pay the costs of war, they become increasingly concerned to know what they are paying for. As Americans begin to play a decisive role in the war, they feel a more vivid sense of responsibility for the outcome and the sequel. So that it is now unusual for any statesman, general, admiral, executive, or other speaker or writer to refer to the war without some allusion to the peace. The minds of all the people of the earth, whether belligerent or neutral, in enemy as well as in friendly nations, are filled not only with a sense of present danger but with hopes and fears of what the distant future has in store.

There are two reasons why this concern for future peace is more intensely and more widely felt than ever before in human history. First, because men see the present war as the penalty paid for the failure of the last, and are resolved not to pay that penalty again. Second, because the rapid shrinkage of the world has made it necessary to organize the whole of the world. This necessity is now so palpable that men have agreed to make it present business.

          ✿   ✿   ✿

Political philosophers have spoken of two conditions of mankind, the "state of nature" in which the relations of men are regulated only by the free exercise of their natural faculties, and the state of civil society in which human relations are regulated by law and government — the second condition being regarded as the remedy for the evils or inconveniences of the first. Until recently, however, there has been a third condition of mankind — the condition, namely, of isolation. It has been possible to solve the problem of human relations, in whole or in part, by the absence of such relations. There was no European-American problem until in the fifteenth century Europe discovered America. The age of discovery was followed by the age of conquest — which was a problem both for the conquerors and for the conquered. For some time afterwards it was possible for Europeans to solve their problems by migrating to America; and even after intercourse between Europe and America was highly developed, remoteness continued to serve as a partial avoidance or solution of their intercontinental problems.

The basic fact governing human relations is that they tend to become harmful unless they are organized. When men come within range of one another, conflicts of interest arise, and these call into play a set of divisive and hostile instincts, such as covetousness, envy, jealousy, rivalry, and combativeness. Conflict can be mitigated or removed by the limitation and redirection of interests; and it can be converted into coöperation by exchange and division of labor. To make the relations of interests innocuous or positively beneficent, instead of destructive and degrading, is what is called morality. Certain forms of this harmonized life are called prudence, temperance, justice, benevolence, veracity, honesty; and these forms of life are happily made possible by reason and reinforced by certain instincts, such as sympathy, love, and consciousness of kind. But so long as ignorance and contrary instincts are not eradicated, some measure of compulsion must be exerted by the whole upon its members. The instruments by which this harmonious adjustment is effected embrace the social institutions, such as custom, education, economy, law, state, and church.[2]

The occasion for morality and its institutions arises, then, wherever men come into contact with one another. It makes not the slightest difference that one man happens to be on the one side and the other on the other side of that invisible line called a boundary. Morality does not stop at the frontier any more than space stops at the frontier. If one man murders, cheats or robs another it is no

---

[2] I omit discussion of the "personal" side of morality, but here also the same principle of harmonious adjustment applies.

less wrong because they happen to be of different races or nations. It would still be "better" if they didn't; and better still if they exchanged goods or pooled their efforts for the good of both. Where there is intercourse there is friction; and where there is friction there is the need of lubrication, and the opportunity of collaboration.

Technological advances have now brought all men into contact with one another, and have thus brought the entire earth's surface into one moral domain and all its inhabitants under one moral jurisdiction. Distance has been annihilated by the development of new means of communication (especially by radio) and of transport (especially by air). Isolation is further impossible, because despite the industrialization of all parts of the world, each industry draws its materials from near and far; and because the increased volume of mass production requires a corresponding increase of purchasing power among all the peoples of the globe. These world-wide human relations require, as the only alternative to that "international jungle"

which Mr. Lawrence Dennis is apparently
prepared to accept,[3] the extension to all mankind of those basic institutions by which
conflicting interests are ordered and harmonized.

There are those who think that it will suffice if this is done in "sections" — a seductive
idea because it sounds moderate and prudent.
Let there be a European peace, and an Anglo-
American peace, and a Far-Eastern peace,
and a Russian peace, and then by adding
these peaces together you will have a world
peace! This idea is also attractive to those
who would have America remain at home —
if not within her strict national frontiers, then
within the boundaries of language or hemi-
spherical geography. It is a new and more
disarming disguise for isolationism.

But sectionalism merely shifts and aggra-
vates the problem. The growth of nation-
states and of alliances has not prevented war,
but has only, by increasing the size of the
warring units, made war more terrible and
destructive. An inter-sectional war might

[3] Cf. his *Dynamics of War and Revolution,* 1940.

well be the final cataclysm before the curtain goes down forever on the tragedy of civilization. There could be no deeper pessimism than the belief that before the world can be at peace it must pass through a phase in which human rivalries and conflicts are consolidated into four gigantic contestants. After such a phase the most probable peace would be a return of man to his prehistoric cave.

If the world were divided into sections, each of which was left to its own devices, what would prevent a conflict of interest among them? What would prevent a more gigantic race of armaments than the world has ever seen? What would prevent the devotion of science to the invention of more destructive instruments of war? What would prevent one section from acquiring illusions of grandeur and seeking to conquer the rest? Surely not a balance of power. For what is to hold such sectional powers in balance? Or what is to prevent three from combining to conquer the fourth? Of all the methods of preserving peace the balance of power should now be the most discredited. A balance of power is at best a temporary and precarious equilibrium of opposing forces, a truce among rivals who are merely biding their time, a momentary pause between the war that is past and the war that is being prepared. And when that war comes, its length and its destructiveness will have been increased, not prevented, by the near-equality of the opponents.

There is one and only one moral solution of this problem, which is to embrace all the nations of the world within one order, supported by a world-wide conscience, enlightened by a world-wide culture, implemented by a world-wide economy, stabilized by world-wide habits, and regulated by world-wide laws under whatever degree or kind of world-wide control may be necessary to create security among the members. This is our proposed solution — the solution for which we fight. And so long as our enemies oppose that solution, as under their present leadership they do, both in thought and in deed, they are wrong and we are right.

✿   ✿   ✿

Morality must be as wide as social institutions. National institutions require a national morality, and world-institutions require a world morality. A nation such as the United States is possible because its inhabitants, on the whole and in the long run, accept the same set of moral ideas. Coercion is undoubtedly necessary, but its role is to bring the abnormal into conformity with the normal. It would be impossible to impose the laws which protect life and property, or which guarantee civil liberties, or which correct injustice, or which prescribe the procedures of democratic government, upon a people that did not adhere by conviction, sentiment, and habit to a common underlying creed: who did not believe in honesty, in the sacredness of life, in the right to use and control the instruments of their happiness, in the right to worship, think, discuss, and persuade, in equality of opportunity, and in the authority of the people who live under the government to determine how and by whom they shall be governed.

It will be noted that this common morality

is far from being the whole of life. It is confined to broad principles, and leaves room for the peculiarities of individuals and of minority groups. It is to be noted, furthermore, that this morality is not coextensive with the sphere of enforcement. The roots of morality, consisting of attitudes and habits, *cannot* be enforced, but must be inculcated by tradition and education; and there are certain practices, such as mendacity, that are so evidently self-defeating that they do not need to be prevented by any other penalties than their own effects. Nor is that public morality which is the condition of the national order coextensive with the *good* life. It provides only the framework within which the higher values of happiness, culture, self-development, piety, friendship, and love may be made possible to the maximum extent for the maximum number of persons.

❀   ❀   ❀

What holds for the nation holds for the world society. World peace and world co-operation cannot be enforced unless there is built up in all nations a firm inner adherence to its underlying principles. This inner adherence cannot be enforced, but must be learned by experience, disseminated by world-wide education, and sustained by a world tradition. Enforcement must confine itself to the overt behavior of nations in their relations to one another. And beyond the limited area of world morality which immediately underlies this prescribed behavior will lie the untouched spheres of purely national life, and all the higher values attainable by persons and nations within the world-wide framework.

*   *   *

The morality which is characteristic of a democratic-Christian society is not only universal in its application, but peculiarly capable of universal adoption.

A liberal or democratic society is that in which the utmost room is made for the private within the public. Liberty, equality, tolerance, self-government, human dignity, all mean, in one way or another, that public regulation shall respect personal choice to the maximum degree which is possible for everybody. Freedom is to be limited only by the requirement of universality — each freedom by its consistency with all freedoms.

This does not imply, as was supposed in the early phase of American democracy, that the functions of government shall be negative: for the development of the individual to the point at which he can choose for himself and do what he chooses, and his protection against the too-free freedoms of others, require the intervention and positive services of government. But the perfected democratic society would be that in which the largest possible sphere of each individual's life was left to the control of his own creative faculties, and in which he encountered both neighbors and the public authorities as allies rather than as obstacles.

A Christian society is a democratic society with added emphasis on the moral foundations of the state, the irreducible reality of the human soul, and the right of that soul to find its spiritual salvation through spiritual agencies independent of the state.

The principles of a democratic Christian

society are thus peculiarly capable of universal extension because they place the minimum of restraint upon the genius and self-regulation of individual nations. The major difficulty of a world polity is its interference with the natural and justifiable desire of each nation to live its own life in its own way. A democratic Christian world polity would not only concede this desire, but assist it in all ways, subject to only one condition, the condition, namely, that it should so express itself in relation to other nations as to permit of their enjoying the same privilege. Such a world polity would ask only one thing of all nations, namely, that they should view the total human situation from the standpoint of all nations, and then act accordingly. That is asking much, it is true; and any given nation could refuse. But it could not refuse on moral grounds, least of all on the general ground of freedom.

The limitations which a democratic Christian *world* order places on nations are much less exacting than those which a democratic Christian national order places on the person

or minority. International behavior is only a
fraction of national behavior, and a still
smaller fraction of the behavior of individual
persons. Similarly, while the world morality
must intersect the lives of all nations and all
persons, it would be but a thin section of their
full concreteness.

*   *   *

How far, then, is it necessary for a world
order to impose a common pattern of thought
and sentiment upon all the world? How far
does it prescribe the way in which the sev-
eral nations shall conduct their own internal
affairs? I am not here concerned with the
question of coercion — undoubtedly a world
order, like a national order, would require
sanctions, and an abandonment of that "absolute" sovereignty which nations are supposed
(questionably) now to possess. But the present question concerns only the extent to
which there must be *agreement* in order that,
when necessary, there can be coercion, and
in order that the nations can dwell together
in relations of peace and mutual help. It

should now be possible to answer that question, if not definitively, then at least in spirit and in principle.

The answer begins by making it clear that a world-wide system of freedom is still a system, and that it is necessary under this as under any other system that the members shall be deeply attached to the system. Moral unity is as necessary for a world polity as for a national polity, and it is as necessary for a democratic Christian polity as for a less liberal polity.

Mr. Myron C. Taylor, who was the President's personal representative at the Vatican, is quoted as having made the following statement at a dinner of the Conference of Christians and Jews in Boston:

"In a broad sense this meeting is a public recognition in America that men of basic faith may dwell together in peace and harmony, to the uplifting of the human family and the glory of God. . . . I am not attracted by the one big family idea. Indeed I am suspicious of the man or woman who has no pride of religion or of race. I cannot con-

vince myself that any world union is possible
in these days if it involves as a prerequisite
the acceptance of a single form of political
economy and government or the acceptance
of a single philosophy. Out of our differences
we have forged our progress." [4]

This, I submit, is an unfortunate statement,
in which the second part appears to contradict the first. "Out of our differences" we
have also forged our wars. If a "basic faith"
is required for peace and harmony at home
it is likewise required for peace and harmony
abroad. The "human family" to be uplifted
is the family of all mankind, and the God to
be glorified is the God of all men. Here is
already the outline of a "single philosophy."

The principles essential to peace must be
accepted and practiced by all who make
peace and keep the peace. Within the broad
framework of these principles there is room
for all those differences which "forge our
progress," and which provide us with many
different prides over and above the common
pride of belonging to the family of mankind.

[4] *Boston Herald,* April 24, 1942.

But this idea of peaceful and enriching differences is itself a basic faith and a single philosophy, which must prevail throughout the world if the world is to enjoy its fruits. Indeed it might be argued that, since the use of force is most difficult in a world polity and most inappropriate in a liberal polity, a liberal world polity must depend more than any other on its moral unity.

What are the elements of that world-wide morality on which all mankind (or most of mankind, most of the time; or the leading and articulate members of mankind) must be persuaded to agree, if a world order is to be possible? What are those habits of thought, feeling, and action which must be generally diffused throughout the peoples of the world if an all-inclusive and harmonious human society is to be stable and enduring?

First, there must be a recognition of duties and obligations to the whole on the part of each nation and its members. It is of the very essence of nationalism, in the sense in which it is an obstacle to world order, that individuals should recognize no obligation save to their own nation. This is the strength of nationalism — its strength for evil: for it gives to individuals a spirit of devotion to an end greater than themselves, but at the same time it moves them to betray an end still greater. It is a partial or pseudo-morality, which is the most dangerous of all enemies to entire and genuine morality.

Second, the obligations imposed by the world order must take precedence of those imposed by the national order, or by personal self-interest. As the personal life must accommodate itself to the limits imposed by the organized nation, so the national life must accommodate itself to the limits imposed by the world order, assuming these limits to be made as wide as possible.

Third, if there is to be a world conscience, in which world obligations are recognized and accepted as paramount, then the influences which create this conscience must be allowed to circulate freely among all men. All men must be allowed to become acquainted with one another's needs, and to profit by one another's experience. All men must enjoy the liberty to think and to speak, and the corresponding liberty to hear and to learn.

Fourth, over and above the cultural expressions peculiar to each nation and of a rich diversity, there must be a cosmopolitan culture embracing the universal values of science, art, and morality.

Fifth, there must be a common love of freedom. By a love of freedom I mean that attitude of mind which finds it equally intolerable to live in subjection and to hold others in subjection. To arouse people from a passive acceptance of tyranny it is only necessary to break their habits, stir their combative emotions and their covetousness, create some symbol of collective action, such as nationalism or racism, and improve their standard of living, so as to give them the hope and the means of improving it further. Nothing is more remarkable than the extent to which this aspiration for freedom has spread to all parts of the world, despite long traditions of servitude. How to arouse people to revolt against tyranny is not the present problem. The difficulty is to prevent a people so aroused, and embittered by the memory of past wrongs, from creating a new tyranny with fresh wrongs to be righted in some future revolt. To stop this cycle of conquest and liberation it is necessary to spread in the world the second and more difficult half of the love of freedom, the half which desires to *give* freedom and not merely claim it.

Sixth, men and nations must feel a sense of joint participation. Liberals are so preoccupied with the escape from tyranny and exploitation that they forget that there is also a deep desire to "escape from freedom." [5] Men must feel that they are marching together to some common destination; that they are not working alone, but that, having done their utmost, they can count on forces greater than themselves to bring the issue to a successful conclusion. Men now find this sense of participation through war, at a fearful cost to themselves and to those other fellow-mortals whom unhappily they must treat as enemies.

Here is the paradox and the tragedy of

[5] Cf. Erich Frome, *Escape from Freedom,* 1941.

human history in a nutshell: that men should find a refuge from their loneliness in the concerted action with which they meet catastrophes of their own creation; that they should have to descend to the level of violence against half of mankind in order to rise to the level of brotherhood with the other half. We must find a better solution of this problem — in a striving all together for the triumph of good over evil and of light over darkness; in the all-inclusive common enterprise of developing to the utmost the resources of physical nature and of the human soul, and distributing the common gains among all the members. Then we may play our parts as free individuals and as free nations, and assume our respective burdens of responsibility, but at the same time feel a double security in the friendship of all other men, and in the irresistible might of the aggregate of men.

*   *   *

Finally, there can be no world order unless all human societies are pervaded by the sentiment of humanity. A world cannot live in peace which is half-humane and half-inhumane. For to the humane inhumanity is intolerable. We rightly hesitate to interfere with the domestic life of our neighbors, but it is impossible to live in proximity to a household in which the wife is beaten by the husband, or the children overworked and starved by the parents, or even in which domestic animals are abused by their owners. Nor can one nation live in proximity to another nation which practices brutality upon its slaves or its minorities. The only valid cause of the American-Spanish War was American sympathy with Cuban victims of Spanish misrule. Sympathy has its own rights over and above the rights of those with whom it sympathizes. And outraged sympathy is a force to be reckoned with. The nazi persecution of the Jews and of the Poles, and the nazi shooting of innocent hostages, have excited among remote American spectators emotions which have played a major part in their willingness to go to war.

There are, I know, those who say that what

others do to others is no concern of ours. Why not close one's eyes and stop one's ears? Why not, like the priest and the Levite of the parable, pass by on the other side?

Because, in a world of press, photography, telegraph, and radio, every cruelty, no matter where it occurs, by whom it is done, and upon whom it is perpetrated, is in the full sight and hearing of every other man. Distance no longer provides a means of evasion, or an escape from pity.

Because one cannot cultivate indifference without becoming like those whose cruelty one condemns. The evidence of men's humanity is the resentment excited in them by inhumanity: the moment inhumanity ceases to excite them they will themselves have become inhumane. And if they feel compassion and resentment they must express them; and if they express them in words they must also act upon them, or they will stand condemned as hypocrites and sentimentalists.

The sentiment of humanity is the ultimate motive and spring of action for any order that would embrace all of humanity. Respect for the dignity of human faculty, concern for the sufferings and joys of human sensibility, sense of kinship with human kind — these are the roots of morality. Their implanting, their cultivation, and their fruition among all peoples is the first condition of a moral order of the world.

NOTE

THE GREATER PART of Chapter I appeared as a letter to the Editor, in the *New York Times*, May 31, 1942. Chapter II was the Winthrop Ames Lecture given at Radcliffe College, March 1, 1942, and first published by Radcliffe College, 1942, under the title: "The World of Tomorrow: Difficulties and Hazards of Democracy." Chapter IV was printed, in substance, in the *Christian Science Monitor*, June 27, 1942. Chapter V was published in part as a letter to the Editor, in the *New York Times*, July 12, 1942.